BEYOND THE
HORIZON

COMBAT AIRCRAFT OF THE NEXT CENTURY

BEYOND THE HORIZON

PHILIP HANDLEMAN

Motorbooks International
Publishers & Wholesalers

DEDICATION

To the next generation of military pilots in the hope that they will never have to fly future combat aircraft for the purpose intended.

This edition first published in 1994 by Motorbooks International, Publishers & Wholesalers, PO Box 2, 729 Prospect Avenue, Osceola, WI 54020, USA.

© Philip Handleman, 1994

Previously published by Airlife Publishing Ltd., Shrewsbury, England, 1994

Library of Congress Cataloging-in-Publication Data is available
ISBN 0-87938-983-X

Printed and bound in Singapore by Kyodo Printing Co. (S'pore) Pte Ltd.

CONTENTS

FOREWORD

by Randall "Duke" Cunningham

I know from my own exposure to aerial combat just how discomfiting it can be to operate antiquated equipment and to serve without proper preparation, so continuing aircraft development is vital. When it comes to the next generation of combat aircraft, the trend is clear. Instead of a wide mix of combat aircraft, the world's air forces will comprise dwindling numbers of aircraft types. Rather than possessing aircraft dedicated to a particular mission, the forces will consist of "multi-role" aircraft designed for a variety of missions.

My old friend, Philip Handleman, has thoroughly researched the coming generation of combat aircraft. Philip describes many of the military planes being contemplated and developed around the world in such depth yet in such an easy-to-understand style that both the professional and the novice will be able to learn and appreciate. The insight that Philip brings to the subject matter comes, in part, from his many years as an active pilot. His opening chapter which provides an overview of what the future may hold for aerial combat is a brilliant analysis that should be required reading for anyone interested in the topic.

AUTHOR'S NOTE

Because future combat aircraft possibilities are infinite, some ground rules had to be adopted for purposes of this book. By and large, the focus is on aircraft that are either in or near prototype form. The book reviews some early stage concepts and a handful of new combat aircraft that have very recently entered operational service. Also included are a few exotic aircraft, presumed to exist, that may have begun flying operational missions.

Combat aircraft, for purposes of this book, are defined to encompass any military planes that might fly in a battlefield scenario. Accordingly, transports are included but trainers are not.

While it is likely that unmanned aerial vehicles will play an increasingly significant role in future air combat, this book's scope is limited primarily to manned aircraft. In those instances where the concept originator has proposed an unmanned variant, it is discussed. Since the book's focus is on a discussion of aircraft, the subject of spacecraft with a military potential is not included.

Heavy reliance on the airframe and component manufacturers for information was necessary for obvious reasons. As the text was being prepared, design changes and test results were announced, requiring manuscript alterations in midstream. With time, there surely will be more changes to the aircraft described in this book. Some may never even go into production or reach operational status for a variety of reasons. The objective has been to describe the world's pending combat aircraft as they exist at a specific point in time.

Instilled with a love of flight from youth, I thrived on illustrated accounts of future planes. I could get lost for hours fantasizing about rides all the way into the upper reaches of the stratosphere at the controls of a sleek, ultra-sophisticated, and tremendously powerful vehicle. Over the years, my curiosity and fascination with future flight have remained robust. I still dream about what looms beyond the horizon.

ACKNOWLEDGEMENTS

Any author attempting to describe the broad range of future combat aircraft must rely on others for assistance. In this meagre space, I would like to express my appreciation to everyone who gave their time and effort in connection with this project. While I am grateful for the help I received, the responsibility for the resulting text is mine alone. Valuable suggestions, information, and photographic materials were provided by the following individuals and organizations: Department of the Air Force; Department of the Navy; Department of the Army; National Aeronautics and Space Administration; Lt-Colonel Howard R. Ebersole, USAF (Ret); Colonel Walter J. Boyne, USAF (Ret); Nixon Galloway; Mark McCandlish; Kerry Leslie; Helen I. Howard, Naval Air Systems Command; Helen A. Kavanaugh, Media Relations, Aeronautical Systems Center, Wright-Patterson AFB; Bobbie Mixon, Jr, Media Relations, Aeronautical Systems Center, Wright-Patterson, AFB; Captain Scot R. Vadnais, Public Affairs, Aeronautical Systems Center, Wright-Patterson AFB; Kristen Liggett, Wright Laboratory, Wright-Patterson AFB; Jim Zeh, Wright Laboratory, Wright-Patterson AFB; Michael Zeigler, Wright Laboratory, Wright-Patterson AFB; Captain Mark O'Hair, Aeronautical Systems Center, Wright-Patterson AFB; Master Sergeant Mary L. Stowe, Public Affairs, USAF; Sergeant Stuart A. Ibberson, Media Relations, Edwards AFB; Nancy Lovato, Public Affairs, NASA Dryden Flight Research Center; Tom Delaney, Public Relations, Westinghouse Electronic Systems; Doug McCurrach, Public Affairs, Martin Marietta Electronic, Information & Missiles Group; Carole E. Jenkins, Public Relations, Pratt & Whitney; J. Thomas Elliott, Engineering & Technology, Pratt & Whitney; Rick Kennedy, Media Relations, GE Aircraft Engines; Ko-Hung Tu, Planning Department, Aero Industry Development Center; Terry Arnold, Tiltrotor Communications, Bell Helicopter Textron Inc.; Robert Torgerson, Communications, Boeing Helicopters Division; Peter Batteu, Public Relations, Westland Group PLC; Jane Oldfield, Press Office, IBM United Kingdom Limited; Isabelle Fleury, Eurocopter S.A.; Christina Gotzhein, Public Relations, Eurocopter Deutschland GmbH; David M. Kamiya, Public Relations, British Aerospace Defence Limited; Wolfram Wolff, Deutsche Aerospace AG; Steve Cox, Boeing Defense and Space Group; Tom Koehler, Public Relations, Boeing Military Airplane Division; Peri Widener, Public Relations, Boeing Military Airplane Division; Joe Stout, Public Affairs, Lockheed Fort Worth Company; Peter G. Hunter, Aircraft Development, Group Vector; Robert A. Slayman, Corporate News and Information, Lockheed Corporation; Ramonda Siniard, Public Relations, Lockheed Aeronautical Systems Company; Richard Stadler, Public Information, Lockheed Advanced Development Company; Denny Lombard, Public Information, Lockheed Advanced Development Company; C. John Amrhein, Visual Communications, Northrop Corporation; Erik Simonsen, Public Relations, Rockwell North American Aircraft; Mark T. Parmenter, Business Development, McDonnell Aircraft Company; Jo Anne Davis, Communications, McDonnell Aircraft Company; Hal Klopper, Public Affairs, McDonnell Douglas Helicopter Company; Bob Williams, Marketing, Scaled Composites; Asa Holm, Public Relations, Saab Military Aircraft; William S. Tuttle, Public Relations, Sikorsky Aircraft; H. J. Dalton, Jr, Corporate Communications, Vought Aircraft Company; Francois Robineau; Katsuhiko Tokunaga; Johnny Lindahl; P. Liander; Ake Anderson; T. Caspersson; Eric Schulzinger.

Most of all, I extend a warm 'thank you' to my wife, Mary, whose understanding and patience during the many hours that I devoted to this project were above and beyond the call of duty.

Below: An imaginary fighter/attack aircraft of the future, this artist's impression features stealthy characteristics like blended engine compartments with contoured inlets on top of the wing. Note that no weapons are carried externally, further minimising the aircraft's radar cross section. The whitish exhaust stream suggests that engines are in afterburner, although it is likely that this plane would have supercruise capability. Nozzles are probably the thrust vectoring type. Foreplanes, known as canards, provide an extra measure of pitch authority, particularly at high angles of attack.

CHAPTER 1
Combat Aircraft of the Future: An Overview

From the beginning of powered flight, aircraft designers have been constrained by their understanding of such specialities as aerodynamics, materials, propulsion, structures, controls, manufacturing technologies, and human factors. Along the way, those broad categories were joined by others like avionics, computation, and, in the case of combat aircraft, weapons systems.

During the last nine decades, the sometimes daunting challenges did not stand in the way of an ongoing progression in aeronautical accomplishment. Invariably, the foundation underlying the advances was imagination. The designers blessed with a vision of the future who willingly incurred risk, incorporating the latest technologies in bold configurations, elevated the state-of-the-art to a new plateau, sometimes startling the world with planes like the P-38 and Me-262 that broke from the conventions of the *status quo*. Performance gains were the ultimate reward.

In the course of air warfare, events have formed perceptions about the direction that designers should take. For example, during the Vietnam War numerous high value targets were heavily defended making aerial attacks both perilous and inaccurate. Efforts at producing precision munitions produced rudimentary laser and electro-optically guided weapons which saw use at the war's end against objectives like Hanoi's Paul Doumer Bridge, a target celebrated for its elusiveness.

The frustration at seeing so many "dumb bombs" fall into the Red River on either side of the bridge like deadweights, only to splash innocuously as U.S. fighter-bomber pilots continually braved a relentless wall of flak, drove designers to devise and then improve air-to-ground weapons systems. The "smart bombs" successfully employed in the 1991 Persian Gulf War owe much of their creation and refinement to the bitter legacy of Vietnam.

The Yom Kippur War of 1973 saw Israel groping to establish a foothold in the air over its primary adversary, Egypt. Unlike the swift victory of just six years earlier in which the Israeli Air Force rapidly achieved a commanding presence in the skies, IAF Phantoms fell prey to newly-deployed Soviet surface-to-air missiles (SAMs). These sophisticated radar-guided weapons caused unacceptably high attrition. Some designers realized that among the counters to this menace would be aircraft with low observables or stealth.

In perhaps the greatest watershed of contemporary air combat history (again in the Middle East where military conceptualists have had their attention drawn repeatedly), the 1982 Bekaa Valley shoot-out, the IAF, pitted against the neighbouring Syrian Air Force, racked up the unprecedented kill/loss ratio of 85/0. This lopsided battle proved that technology affords the means to surmount the SAM threat and, further, that control of the electronic environment in the modern air war is the key to victory. The fruits of this doctrine materialized on a grand scale less than ten years later with the stunning success of the coalition's air campaign in the Persian Gulf War.

Achieving air superiority has long been recognized as a prime early objective in battle. Much of the responsibility for this falls on the shoulders of the fighter force. Until fairly recently, air-to-air combat remained fundamentally unchanged since the days of World War I dogfighting, where one-on-one aerial duels ensued, an aircraft chasing another in the wild manoeuvring above a seemingly detached battlefield. Success hinged on a plethora of factors including the pilot's eyesight, reflexes, experience, training, and airmanship. A less easily defined factor, termed situational awareness, also has continued

9

to play a major role in determining the outcome of air fighting.

Naturally, the aircraft and its weapons systems can greatly tilt the balance. Speed, climb performance, and, perhaps most importantly, agility, were the characteristics sought by fighter pilots. Being able to out-turn or out-run an enemy made the difference between life and death in what was evolving from a chivalrous endeavour into a bloody business.

Protective shielding was an attractive feature though virtually non-existent in the early days. Intelligently designed camouflage paint schemes provided a measure of cover. Devices for escape like parachutes were at first scoffed at by the hierarchy of some air forces as inherently cowardly. Having forward-firing synchronized machine-guns offered Germany a significant advantage until the other side could match this technology. Sheer quantity was another factor; attaining higher production rates and fielding the growing fleets of aircraft could swamp the enemy.

The main goal of today's fighter aircraft designers is to devise a plane that can counter the threat from afar, obviating the need to engage in old-style dogfighting while at the same time not diminishing, perhaps even enhancing, the traditional values just in case. This means developing aircraft that on the one hand are invisible to the enemy but on the other hand that can ideally strike the threat at beyond visual range (BVR).

Lowering an aircraft's observables is most important in the radar spectrum, since, of all sensors, radar's range is the greatest. Additionally, the infrared (IR), visual, and acoustic signatures must be reduced. The first full-fledged stealth aircraft, the F-117A, using early-generation stealth technology was comprised of a faceted structure. Current generation stealth technology is going into the B-2, which is a flying wing devoid of customary tail surfaces and possessing smooth, curving shapes. Radar-absorbing materials (RAMs) like carbon fibreglass are part of the structure.

The future fighter will be stealthy, avoiding detection by both air and ground threats. Engines will be blended into the fuselage. Air inlets may be specially treated or inset and the exhaust stream will be shielded in some fashion. There will be no smoke or contrails. Sound will be muffled unless, of course, still in the atmosphere the aircraft exceeds Mach 1, at which point the unavoidable sonic boom occurs. All fuel and weapons carriage will be internal or conformal so as not to contribute to radar reflectivity. Refuelling probes will be retractable or receptacles will be covered.

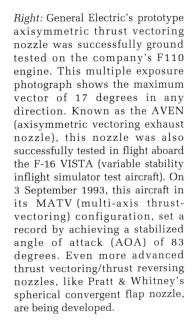

Right: General Electric's prototype axisymmetric thrust vectoring nozzle was successfully ground tested on the company's F110 engine. This multiple exposure photograph shows the maximum vector of 17 degrees in any direction. Known as the AVEN (axisymmetric vectoring exhaust nozzle), this nozzle was also successfully tested in flight aboard the F-16 VISTA (variable stability inflight simulator test aircraft). On 3 September 1993, this aircraft in its MATV (multi-axis thrust-vectoring) configuration, set a record by achieving a stabilized angle of attack (AOA) of 83 degrees. Even more advanced thrust vectoring/thrust reversing nozzles, like Pratt & Whitney's spherical convergent flap nozzle, are being developed.

Left: The NF-15B Short Take-off and Landing/Manoeuvre Technology Demonstrator (S/MTD) using thrust vectoring nozzles and canards achieved a 38 percent reduction in the runway length normally required for take-off and a reduction of more than two-thirds in the runway length normally required for landing. Moreover, higher angles of attack were achieved during inflight manoeuvres. Thrust reversers were used in flight to decelerate from supersonic speeds. An onboard Autonomous Landing Guidance system permitted a no-lights precision landing. The plane's toughened landing gear allows taxiing over rough surfaces.

Carrying packages of sophisticated sensors, the future fighter should be able to detect enemy fighters at BVR. An electronically-scanned antenna will replace the traditional movable antenna. IR sensors will be mounted internally rather than located in a pod affixed to a wing or fuselage stores station. These IR sensors will have greatly improved range and provide vastly enhanced imagery. Laser technology will be employed as part of the targeting system. Connected by two-way data link to airborne and ground stations, the fighter will be able to receive valuable input about enemy targets from deployed forces.

As the threat aircraft attempts to locate the future fighter, active jamming may be undertaken using onboard systems to intercept and purposefully deflect the enemy's incoming radar signals. In this way, the future fighter is not dependent upon dedicated electronic countermeasures (ECM) aircraft. The future fighter has a full bag of tricks before it is relegated to dispensing chaff or flares to survive.

In any full-blown combat scenario, air bases will have been struck and runways most likely will be damaged, dramatically limiting usable length. To address this concern, the future fighter must have thrust vectoring nozzles that give it short take-off and landing (STOL) capability.

An exciting variation is the advanced short take-off and vertical landing (ASTOVL) fighter. Loaded with fuel and ordnance it will be too heavy to take-off vertically, but with an advanced propulsion system could take-off in an extremely short roll. Landing could easily be accomplished vertically. The ASTOVL ought to be able to approximate the speed and manoeuvrability of its conventional counterparts. Another challenge is to preserve acceptable fuel and weapons payloads given the necessary extra weight and volume for the vectoring apparatus.

The future fighter at first may have two-dimensional thrust vectoring nozzles. Testing is now being done on axisymmetric thrust vectoring nozzles that will enhance yaw and pitch manoeuvrability. Not only will there be short take-off capability because of these engine nozzles, but air combat manoeuvring capability will be expanded.

The future fighter will be able to achieve higher angles of attack (AOA) as a result of vectoring engine thrust. During close-in air-to-air combat this provides an immense advantage. Being able to vector thrust through a wide envelope effectively transforms engine nozzles into steering devices. This development could lead to tail-less aircraft configurations that enjoy an intrinsic stealthiness.

Opposite: The X-29, conceived as a testbed for forward swept wing research, was fitted with small nose-mounted thrusters towards the end of its flight test programme in 1992. With this enhancement, the X-29 achieved controllable flight at higher angles of attack. Pictured is the X-29 at about 25 degrees AOA during a vortex flow visualisation test on 10 September 1991. Tracking the smoke emanating from the nose helps to evaluate the research plane's high alpha characteristics.

Adding still more to the future fighter's high AOA capabilities could be small nose-mounted thrusters able to push the aircraft beyond its normal stall departure point and continue to provide reasonable control at those high alpha attitudes. Flight testing of this concept was successfully accomplished on the X-29 forward-swept wing research aircraft.

Flying at supersonic speeds without the use of afterburner, known as supercruise, will give the future fighter better fuel economy, greater range, and a lower IR signature. Afterburner will be available for times of need when, for example, rapid acceleration is dictated. Greater thrust-to-weight ratios will improve performance. Full authority digital electronic controls (FADEC) can provide unprecedented responsiveness. Continuous health monitoring will pinpoint engine problems before they become critical.

Materials in the construction of aircraft structures have increasingly moved from customary metal alloys to composites like carbon fibre. Quite simply, composites tend to offer more strength while weighing less. Their toughness means they are ballistics tolerant. Moreover, composites are more corrosion resistant. This is a critical consideration as corrosion is a leading cause of maintenance difficulties. Combat aircraft, by the very nature of their missions, are exposed to inhospitable surroundings. Composites can contribute to a longer service life with lower maintenance requirements.

The weight savings permit more onboard fuel which translates into increased range or endurance. More payload can be devoted to weaponry and mission-related gear. Being lighter, the aircraft should be more manoeuvrable.

Rather than attaching or incorporating essential equipment on or in the shell of the airframe as is traditional, the equipment may become an integral part of the aircraft structure. For example, an integrated antenna might be embedded into the contour of the fuselage, in effect, making it a "smart structure".

Smart structures and smart skins have wide-ranging utility. Examples include a sensor-laden wing that could report battle damage or even age-related fatigue. Engineers are investigating the practicality of producing structures with electro-rheological fluids injected as a constant monitoring agent that would automatically sense, measure, and signal the extent and location of structural changes occurring in flight. Aware of combat-incurred difficulties, the smart structures would automatically reconfigure flight controls and redistribute loads to optimize aircraft performance until major repairs could be made.

The crew station will have a glass cockpit. Data from the complex systems will funnel through microprocessors and be presented on three or four flat panel multifunction displays (MFDs). The presentation will take the form of easily comprehended graphics. So as not to overload the pilot, at any point during the flight only relevant data or data specifically called up by the pilot would be presented. Sensor data will be fused and presented on the few displays in an overlapping format.

Simple push button mode switches will configure the displays for the current flight regime, for example, take-off, cruise, combat, and landing. If any system malfunction occurs, a warning feature automatically engages, alerting the pilot. A suggested course of action may accompany the annunciator read-out.

Complementing or possibly replacing the holographic head-up display (HUD), which projects vital data and allows the pilot to literally keep his head up, looking out through the windscreen, will be a lightweight helmet-mounted display (HMD) incorporating its own HUD-like device. No matter which direction the pilot turns, the same crucial flight and combat data will travel with his helmet visor, never leaving his sight.

The "in-helmet" symbology will be standardized with the MFD symbology. Certain presentations may even have a three dimensional appearance, enhancing situational awareness. The HMD will also be compatible with night vision systems.

When sensors detect an enemy plane, a data card describing the actual threat aircraft may be called up from the future fighter's data base. The display may be accompanied by stereoscopic three dimensional warning tones originating from the direction of the threat. This kind of acoustic cuing enhances situational awareness.

As the future fighter manoeuvres into appropriate position, a new anti-G suit will inflate giving the pilot added tolerance. The hand grip on the control stick will contain many carefully-designed buttons and switches whose functions will be readily comprehensible. Just by feel, the pilot will know what system he is activating with his fingertips.

Nevertheless, as G-forces build, pilot hand movements become increasingly laborious. In the future cockpit, the pilot need only announce his command verbally. A cockpit computer will have been pre-programmed with the pilot's "voice footprint". With a voice command like "fire" or "launch", the pilot would activate his weapons.

Pictorials such as recently-taken reconnaissance photographs may be displayed with overlapping moving maps and highlighted rings depicting ranges. An onboard computer may quickly generate life-like images of the proposed ground target from assembled data. The picture may be presented from various angles. Simulated bomb runs with projected enemy air defences will be displayed as well, with an onboard system, reliant upon artificial intelligence, calculating the least hazardous and most effective flight profile.

Since the entry of the F-16 into service there has been the expectation that future fighters will, like the Falcon, have redundant fly-by-wire (FBW) flight control

Below: In an effort to improve performance of future fighters (as well as assist in the design of new high speed civil transports), NASA is conducting a research programme using the F-16XL to investigate laminar flow at supersonic speeds. By minimising the turbulent layer across the airfoil, reductions in aerodynamic drag and fuel consumption can be achieved. The cranked-arrow delta wing of this modified two-seat F-16 has double the wing area of a standard F-16. As a result, 80 percent more fuel can be carried, vastly extending range.

systems (FCSs). The pilot manipulates the control stick and computers read the input, transferring a measured force to an actuator that moves the appropriate control surface just the right amount to achieve the desired effect. These systems are lighter weight and less prone to battle damage. They can be programmed to prevent the aircraft from entering unrecoverable flight attitudes.

Avionics advances over the last 40 years have probably outpaced progress in other aviation-related technologies. From vacuum tubes to transistors to microchips, the modern fighting plane can process and integrate large inputs of data. The current focus is on very high speed integrated circuit (VHSIC) technology. Computers based on VHSIC technology are faster, smaller, lighter, and more reliable.

Silicon, the well-known computer chip material, may give way to gallium arsenide, which offers even more improved performance. But the real revolution around the corner is in fibre optics, also known as photonics. Eventually, much electronic hardware will be replaced by photonic devices, which, using lasers, will directly transmit huge volumes of data at the speed of light. With optical signal processing, no longer will there be the intermediate steps of breaking down sensor- gathered data into digital code and then reassembling the pieces in comprehensible form for transmission.

Photonics technology promises to foster fly-by-light (FBL) flight control systems. These will weigh less and consume less energy than FBW systems. A major advantage of photonic devices is that they are immune to electronic jamming as well as radiation and the electromagnetic effects in the aftermath of a nuclear explosion.

Any future fighter, no matter how sophisticated in itself, will not gain a net advantage in the air battle unless its weaponry has kept pace with the plane's technology. Having a stealthy, super-cruising, thrust-vectoring fighter whose pilot is relegated to using short range or unreliable air-to-air missiles, requiring visual contact with the threat aircraft, negates much of the benefits

from the advances incorporated in the airframe.

Not long ago, the AIM-120 AMRAAM (advanced medium range air-to-air missile) was introduced into the operational inventory and was used to enforce "no-fly zones" over portions of Iraq. This is a radar-guided missile intended to replace the sometimes controversial old standby, the AIM-7 Sparrow.

In part, because of AMRAAM's microminiaturized solid state electronics, it weighs approximately one-third less than the Sparrow. In live-fire tests of 128 missiles, AMRAAM proved more reliable than its predecessor.

Capable of engaging the enemy at BVR day or night, in any weather, AMRAAM uses its own guidance system, updated before launch by systems aboard the fighter, to midcourse. At this juncture, the missile can be further updated from the fighter's radar via data link. Then the missile's nose-mounted radar seeker alone provides guidance to the target. The solid rocket motor propels AMRAAM supersonically, but produces only a minimal smoke plume so as not to visually alert the opponent.

AMRAAM may be fired at multiple targets in rapid succession. It is also better protected against ECM. This kind of weapon, operating in a consistently reliable manner in the real-world environment, is absolutely imperative for the other technologies of the future fighter to be meaningful.

Ongoing goals include development of air-to-air weapons that are exceedingly accurate with even longer ranges and that have true "fire and forget" capability. Multiple lock-ons with simultaneous firing is important as well since the future fighter may find itself confronted by many bogeys at once. Trying to maximize kills per pass is the overriding objective. Chances of retaliatory launches are thereby diminished.

For all the high-tech gadgetry going into new fighters, there is, of course, the possibility that the perimeter of sophistication will be pierced. In such a

15

Below: Wright-Patterson Air Force Base in Dayton, Ohio is home to the Aeronautical Systems Center and the Wright Laboratory. These facilities conduct much of the U.S. military's research into future flight. The cockpit of the future is being developed there. A simulator called MAGIC (microcomputer application of graphics and interactive communications) is used to test concepts for the cockpit of the future. Experiments include voice-activated commands, three-dimensional colour displays, stereoscopic acoustic cuing, pictorial data storage and retrieval, and touch-sensitive controls using an ultra-sonic hand tracker worn as a glove that is essentially a three-dimensional mouse.

scenario, the encounter will quickly degenerate into an old-fashioned dogfight. Therefore, more prosaic weapons like close-in heat-seeking air-to-air missiles (for example, the Sidewinder) and internally-mounted guns have an important backup role. The fighter pilot must retain the type of air combat manoeuvring skills first demonstrated during World War I. It would be a mistake at any time in the near future to remove from the fighter pilot curriculum the training associated with this kind of flying.

For cost and safety reasons a greater percentage of training will occur in advanced motion simulators where, utilizing virtual reality, computer generated images will present an amazingly accurate portrayal of the real-world environment. Only the press of G-forces will be absent in these realistic simulators.

Air-to-ground ordnance has a way to go in continuation of the revolution that has dramatically increased point accuracy. Precision munitions, often called smart bombs, are being developed that will require fewer sorties per target. Advances in IR, millimetre wave, and laser radar technologies will improve detection, identification, tracking, and guidance. For example, the future attack aircraft's pilot, during the attack, will not have to hold on target directing laser energy until impact. Immediately following launch, the weapon will streak to the target under a completely autonomous guidance system. To prevent intercept, the weapon itself will have a stealthy design.

Such weapons will have greatly expanded range so as to keep the attacking aircraft and its crew out of harm's way. Warhead-free very high velocity missiles launched from high altitude where anti-

aircraft artillery is unable to reach, will rely completely on their energy for destructive force. Hardened targets would not be safe. The extreme speed of these missiles will make them troublesome to intercept.

A new class of weapon is being developed. Known as non-destructive weapons, they would disable vital segments of a warring power's infrastructure without causing permanent or irreversible damage. For example, electrical facilities might be crippled temporarily by interfering with electromagnetic fields. Runways would not be destroyed, but put out of service for the war's duration by spreading super slippery or adhesive agents to their surfaces.

Because of harsh economic realities, military planners are having to confront, with heightened intensity, the age-old issue of quantity versus quality. It would be possible, for example, to buy several F-16s off the production line for the price of a single F-22. While the issue does not always require an "either/or" decision, consideration must be given to the changing geopolitical outlook, the kinds of battles that may crop up, and the prospective sophistication of the future threat.

With the defence budgets of the major industrial powers being scaled back there is increasing pressure on the design community to create airframes with multirole capabilities rather than airframes for a lone dedicated mission. Historically, more than a few attempts to design several tasks into a particular plane, making it a "jack of all missions", resulted in an aircraft that performed none of its assignments in an exemplary manner.

Current scarce funding leaves little alternative but to "double up" capabilities. As an example, the F-22 had its original design purpose expanded from solely air-to-air combat to both air-to-air combat and ground attack. Designers, therefore, face a stiff challenge, looking for ways to squeeze more versatility out of their necessarily better performing aircraft.

Another probable impact of declining defence spending is more emphasis on

retrofitting and upgrade programmes. Aircraft that were constrained to good weather and daytime missions, can perform more effectively in an expanded window of opportunity with the addition of systems developed after the aircraft were designed, like F-16s fitted with LANTIRN (Low Altitude Navigation and Targeting Infrared for Night) systems. The flight envelope of older designs, again like F16s, can be significantly enhanced through installation of thrust vectoring nozzles on their existing engines. These kinds of modifications to planes already in the inventory help modernize an ageing fleet at relatively low costs.

Development and production costs have risen dramaticaly and have become prohibitive. Whereas in years past military planes were built for a short service life, future combat aircraft will have to last for periods of up to 50 years. To be useful for such a long time, the design will have to allow for technological growth.

Because relatively small numbers of these aircraft can be afforded, they must meet stringent reliability standards. Attrition rates of yesteryear are unacceptable. During World War II, the Allies operated tens of thousands of heavy bombers, but in the emerging environment with, for example, a total U.S. long-range heavy bomber force of just over 100 aircraft, the loss of even a single plane represents a substantial percentage

Above: High altitude, high speed aircraft that outclass the 1960's vintage SR-71 Blackbird are rumoured to be flying on operational missions. Supposedly capable of altitudes approaching 150,000 feet and speeds in excess of Mach 5, these aircraft, as in this artist's concept, may have a sleek clipped delta plantorm. Design purpose is on-demand reconnaissance in an untouchable flight regime. Perhaps there is in this remarkable penetrator an offensive capability as well.

reduction in the force and a "dent" that is felt.

The often espoused concept of jointness now has come of age. The funding environment requires that the services meld their programmes, resulting wherever feasible in the same aircraft for navy and air force. It is no coincidence that the Rafale is going to both the Armée de l'Air and the Aéronautique Navale. If inter-service rivalries can be suppressed, this change will produce positive results.

In the private sector, there is already an industry-wide march toward joint venturing. Because the stakes are so high and developmental costs so great, many companies have decided to share the risks associated with new aircraft programmes.

Competitions for lucrative contracts have already become, by and large, contests among teams of the remaining handful of large airframe manufacturers. In the sometimes convoluted world of the aerospace business, team members can actually compete against themselves. As an example, Lockheed at one point belonged to four of the five teams bidding for the ill-fated A/F-X.

Teaming arrangements have even spanned national borders. Eurofighter 2000 is evolving from a four-nation consortium. The X-31 Enhanced Fighter Man-oeuvrability programme is a joint effort of Rockwell in the U.S. and Germany's Deutsche Aerospace. Even the design bureaux of the former Soviet Union, at the moment reportedly strapped for cash, have let it be known that they will entertain joint ventures with their Western counterparts. With the longstanding danger of the two traditional superpowers colliding in a nuclear conflagration now consigned to memory, the focus of coming joint ventures, including those between East and West, will be on designs for conventional as opposed to nuclear warfare.

The increasing corporate amalgamation occurring in the face of an ever-diminishing number of new aircraft programmes has fostered a shift from design with a highly individualistic imprint to design by committee. Bureaucracy is noted for stifling creativity, so enlightened corporate managers will have to guard against this phenomenon. Perhaps periodic reminders of the success of the Lockheed Skunk Works, a semi-independent think-tank/workshop with a lean staff possessed of a can-do attitude and led by an insightful, decisive executive imbued with uncommon authority, would serve the industry well.

An inescapable problem resulting from the current state of affairs is that the centres of creativity are inexorably dwindling. Companies like Martin, Curtiss, and Fairchild, to name a few, that produced unforgettable combat aircraft, no longer design and build whole aircraft. Some of the remaining airframe manufacturers have gone on acquisition binges, gobbling up competitors, such that precious few sources for new combat aircraft are left. The multitude of sources from the vibrant industry of the past virtually assured that the right plane would emerge at the right time. Now and in the future there will be no margin for error.

In a paradoxical twist, lead times have grown geometrically. Half a century ago it was possible to take a promising idea like the P-80 from letter of intent to first flight in little more than six months. By contrast, the development of the F-22 has taken the better part of a decade from configuration concept to maiden flight of the demonstrators. This future fighter will start entering service in the latter half of the 1990s at the earliest.

Incredible design and manufacturing technologies have been developed without which future combat aircraft would simply not be buildable. Yet for all the advances such as computer-aided design/computer-aided manufacturing (CAD/CAM) and computational fluid dynamics (CFD), lead times are far longer. It is ironic that with the tools of modern technology, current lead times for combat aircraft development drastically exceed the lead times from the days of drafting tables and slide rules.

Of course, there are differences between then and now. The military today expects

Opposite: This conception of a "smart weapon" ferreting out and striking hidden mobile targets is based on a multi-sensor target recognition system. Both forward-looking infrared (FLIR) and millimetre wave multimode radar sensors are incorporated in the forward section of this unmanned, self-propelled, air-breathing weapon. Sensor data are instantly analysed by an onboard computer capable of performing 86 billion operations per second. Upon verification, the mother weapon dispenses precision-guided munitions that attack the high value targets only. Note in this depiction that the precision-guided munitions are surgically knocking out mobile missile launchers, such as those used to transport the infamous SCUD missiles, while the attack aircraft that launched the smart weapon is not even in sight.

its planes to have much longer service lives than used to be the case. Tolerances must be much greater. For example, the B-2 Stealth bomber's 172-foot wing span is accurate to within a quarter of an inch, a tolerance unattainable at any prior time. Combat aircraft are being called upon to do more: supercruise stealthily or fly like a plane/land like a helicopter. The high price tags make popular support and the corresponding governmental support erratic. Efforts to hide details of known programmes under the cloak of national security generally exacerbate the problem.

In the final analysis, lead times are a function of user need. When a nation is desperate, its industries throw out the book of accepted practices and exhibit ingenuity. Under such circumstances, people are motivated and jobs get done in unprecedented time with a higher level of quality. During World War II, despite the relentless battering sustained by German factories, aircraft production continued. It was the depletion of fuel that fatally handicapped the Luftwaffe.

The latent spirit that can cut lead times is still alive. During the Persian Gulf War, standard protocol was abandoned in a number of instances. An obscure but promising electronic warfare system still undergoing testing was pressed into service. Thus, the E-8 Joint/STARS (Joint Surveillance and Target Attack Radar System) proved an invaluable asset in the prosecution of the air campaign, providing a level of intelligence about enemy ground movements never before available to military commanders. Similarly, the U.S. Air Force rapidly responded to the need for an oversize smart bomb. Disregarding normal development channels, two 4,700 lb laser-guided GBU-28 weapons were successfully deployed as bunker busters. Iraq accepted ceasefire terms the next day.

There seems to be universal agreement that the future battlefield, in all its dimensions, will be increasingly lethal. Effectively commanding forces in such an environment will require real-time and near real-time intelligence disseminated directly to end users. There must also be improvements in the pace and accuracy of bomb damage assessment (BDA). These burdens will fall to a disproportionate degree on specialized reconnaissance aircraft.

Increasing reliance for real-time and near real-time intelligence has been placed on unmanned aerial vehicles (UAVs). The success of early generation remotely piloted vehicles (RPVs) in the 1982 Bekaa Valley battle, in which the IAF deftly employed their drones as decoys to lure hostile SAM batteries to give away their positions, encouraged other countries to pursue UAV technology with renewed vigour.

The effective utilization of UAVs has rekindled debate over whether or not manned aircraft will be necessary or prudent in the years to come. Indeed, moves away from man-in-the-cockpit have already occurred. The Tomahawk land attack missile, in a sense a more sophisticated version of the V1 and V2 weapons of World War II, is a pre-programmed cruise missile that once launched guides itself to the target. The Patriot missile intercepts aerial targets.

UAVs definitely have some advantages over manned aircraft. The most obvious is that they remove the pilot from exposure to possible hazard. They can usually loiter for longer durations than piloted aircraft. Being smaller, they are less expensive. Also, they are less complex and easier to maintain.

Yet, those who forecast the phase-out of manned fighters many years ago were premature. Even now, with enormous strides in technology, most missions require an onboard pilot or pilots. Further, even if the pilot were removed from the cockpit, he would still have to fly the aircraft during battle from a remote station. There would at least be man-in-the-loop, though at some distance.

By being so far removed from the action, the pilot would suffer from the narrow confines of the tactical situation relayed by the plane's sensors. Only by being on the scene may the pilot react to correct problems using his unmatched reasoning powers. Until technology can address the limitations of UAVs, man-in-the cockpit seems destined to remain an integral aspect of combat flying.

It was perhaps to be expected that as air combat became more sophisticated with speeds and altitudes climbing in a kind of upward spiral, a push into space would occur. When man started to venture into this last frontier, many hoped that space would somehow retain its purity. While it still may not be too late, there are, in addition to spy satellites already in orbit, inklings of exotic planes flying so high and so fast that no SAM can touch them or for that matter even detect them.

In pondering the dazzling advances that have occurred in aerospace technologies and how these may find application in future combat aircraft it is easy to get, no pun intended, carried away. It is important to remember that all the high-tech gadgetry in the world will not replace the heart of the dedicated military pilot. Assuming the requisites of experience, training, and flying skill, the combat pilot who believes in his cause and is motivated gives added dimension to his sophisticated aircraft. High-tech, after all, is only as good as the people manipulating it.

Opposite: Escalating costs and declining defence budgets will mean extensive upgrades to the aging fleet of existing combat aircraft. The Low Altitude Navigation and Targeting Infrared for Night (LANTIRN) system, consisting of two externally mounted pods, is an example of the add-ons that can enhance the combat capabilities of older fighters. This flight test F-16 has the two LANTIRN pods, one for navigation and the other for targeting, mounted just below the engine air inlet. LANTIRN sensors enable safe low-level flight, day or night, in any weather and the acquisition, tracking, and striking of ground targets with increased accuracy. The pods can be used independently of one another based on mission requirements. In addition to the LANTIRN pods, this F-16 is carrying Maverick air-to-ground missiles, Sidewinder air-to-air missiles, and external fuel tanks. Sophisticated future fighters will be designed to carry all weapons-related systems internally or conformally.

21

CHAPTER 2
Lightning II: Advanced Tactical Fighter

Opposite: The U.S. Air Force's YF-22A prototype advanced tactical fighter (ATF) underwent an extensive flight test programme in a dem/val phase and later in an EMD phase. As can be seen from this angle that exposes the overhead planform, the aircraft has constant chord wing leading edge flaps. There are outboard ailerons and inboard flaperons along the trailing edges of a modified diamond wing. Tail surfaces are twin canted vertical stabilisers with constant chord rudders and all-moving clipped diamond stabilators. Ensuring stealthiness, all exterior edge angles are swept so as to align with the sweep of either the wing leading or trailing edge. Refuelling receptacle can be seen on the upper fuselage midway between the cockpit and the engine nozzles.

The U.S. Air Force's next generation fighter evolved from the work of a tripartite corporate venture headed by Lockheed whose prolific design offices have created such superlative fighters as the World War II P-38 Lightning. Originally teamed with the Lockheed Aeronautical Systems Company were the Boeing Military Airplane Company and the General Dynamics Fort Worth Division (which, in 1993 was acquired by Lockheed Corporation, becoming the Lockheed Fort Worth Company).

This teaming arrangement took shape in June 1986. Each of the three team partners had pursued its own design concepts for the Air Force's proposed advanced tactical fighter (ATF). Lockheed's first design concepts for this future fighter were generated from 1982 to 1985. Refinements in the selected aircraft configuration were made through the time of the teaming arrangement. Revisions to reduce supersonic drag were required later.

On 31 October, 1986, the enormous commitment of the team partners, especially Lockheed, to research in aerodynamics, materials, avionics, and human factors paid off. The Air Force that day announced that its competition for the ATF had been narrowed down to two contractor teams: the venture headed by Lockheed and another headed by Northrop in partnership with McDonnell Douglas. Both teams were expected to build and fly two prototypes of their ATF designs as part of the project's demonstration/valuation (dem/val) phase.

The two teams brought great talent to the competition. Significantly, McDonnell Douglas produced the service's current air superiority fighter, the F-15 Eagle. Lockheed's prototype was designated the YF-22A and Northrop's prototype was designated the YF-23A.

Following a rigorous review of the two competing designs, including analysis of the flight test data accumulated in the 'fly-off' between the prototypes, the Air Force gave its nod to Lockheed's entry, the Lightning II. Selected at the same time was an advanced powerplant, Pratt & Whitney's new F119 engine.

The Northrop YF-23 was a highly regarded competitor, and no doubt, if chosen, would have been a splendid ATF. The Secretary of the Air Force had to admit that the decision was difficult given the outstanding performance of both competing prototypes.

While much of the data gathered during the fly-off are still classified, the consensus among informed observers is that the YF-23 excelled in low observables (stealth) but that when it came to the classic fighter characteristic of manoeuvrability, the YF-22 carried the day. The YF-22 was said to be less costly to maintain, a consideration that had increased importance given the impending severe defence budget cuts. Also, it seemed that the Lockheed team's leadership was less risk averse in its overall approach, including the flight test programme.

When the production version, the F-22, enters service it will be the most advanced air superiority fighter the world has ever seen. It will possess a combat capability in excess of any known threat into the first and perhaps the second decade of the next century.

The F-22 promises to be far more stealthy than any fighter aircraft in history. This attribute will shield the F-22 from early detection by enemy fighters. Because of its own powerful onboard sensors, it will enjoy a greater beyond visual range (BVR) air-to-air combat capability and the advantages of first look/first shot.

Its low observables across many spectra will also enable it to effectively perform ground attack missions like Lockheed's

Above: Agility is a key feature of this next generation fighter. Perceived as vastly superior to any current or postulated fighter, the F-22 should be able to out-manoeuvre any anticipated threat well into the future. Its stealth combined with powerful sensors should, however, prevent the F-22 from having to engage in the classic close-in dogfight. The aircraft's superior design and systems will give it extraordinary beyond visual range (BVR) capability so that enemy fighters can be fired upon without warning. The element of surprise will give the F-22 an advantage in air-to-air combat.

Right: The F-22 will be powered by two Pratt & Whitney F119-PW-100 afterburning engines. However, these very high thrust-to-weight ratio engines can provide the aircraft with supersonic speeds without use of afterburner. This is known as supercruise. The engines have two-dimensional thrust vectoring nozzles which improve the aircraft's short field capabilities and enhance manoeuvrability. Indeed. the YF-22 achieved controllable flight at 60 degrees AOA. All fuel is carried internally unless the aircraft is being ferried long distances. The aerodynamic blending, supercruise feature, and comparative fuel efficiency provide for greater combat radius and time on station than current air superiority fighters.

F-117A Stealth fighter. (The F-22 was designed as an air superiority fighter exclusively, but with reduced defence spending a multi-role capability is now assured of being developed.) In the air superiority configuration, all the F-22's weapons and fuel will be carried internally.

Newly-developed Pratt & Whitney F119 engines will give the F-22 the ability to cruise at supersonic speeds without use of afterburner. This so-called supercruise feature provides high speed at a relatively efficient fuel burn rate. If required for quick acceleration, afterburner may be used. The F-22's thrust-to-weight ratio will exceed that of the F-15.

Two-dimensional trust vectoring nozzles (with a capability of 20 degrees up or down), the aerodynamics of its diamond-shaped wing and four tail surfaces, and the advanced digital fly-by-wire flight control system will imbue the F-22 with unsurpassed maneuvrability. Indeed, one of the prototypes achieved controllable flight at a 60 degree angle of attack. Thus, if an enemy fighter should happen to penetrate the F-22's defensive outer perimeter, the F-22 can out-manoeuvre the intruder during close-in air-to-air combat.

The F-22 is expected to possess vastly improved short field take-off and landing capabilities recognizing the probability of having to operate from battle-damaged runways. Combat radius of the F-22 will be greatly expanded beyond current fighters, reducing inflight refuelling requirements. This will allow the F-22 to carry the fight

Below: Flight testing of the prototype YF-22 included aerial refuelling. Here, the refuelling boom of an Air Force KC-135 connects with the demonstrator's receptacle.

to enemy airspace, containing much of the air threat to a limited arena. Sortie generation rates should increase by a factor of one and a half over those of the F-15.

Reliability, maintainability, serviceability, and supportability of the F-22 are all supposed to be significantly improved over the F-15. For example, there is projected to be a 30 per cent reduction in squadron manpower because of the lower maintenance requirements of the F-22. Direct maintenance man-hours are expected to shrink by 50 per cent. A doubling of overall reliability is anticipated.

Very high speed integrated circuit (VHSIC) technology will be extensively incorporated into the F-22's avionics. Data will be rapidly transmitted via high-speed data buses, providing multi-colour graphics on fusion liquid crystal displays (LCDs). The integration of data incoming from various sensors and their overlapped presentation in the form of easily comprehensible symbology on user-friendly displays will minimize pilot workload and maximize pilot performance.

The integrated avionics system will employ a minimum number of common modules, superseding current "black box" technology. The F-22's software for the

Pave Pillar avionics architecture is being written in the Ada computer language, mandated by the U.S. Department of Defence. Use of Ada will provide commonality with other new programmes.

Avionics will include the integrated electronic warfare system (INEWS) and integrated communications/ navigation/ identification avionics (ICNIA). The promising technology of fibre optics will be utilized for data transmission. Low-observable antennas will not be single-purpose dedicated, but have shared uses.

The objectives of the current engineering and manufacturing development (EMD) phase of the F-22 programme have been made all the more reachable because of the aggressive dem/val phase which included the accumulation of 91.6 flight hours in 74 flights by the two prototypes over a 91-day flight test period. During the flight tests, the prototypes achieved supercruise, successfully launched both an AIM-9 Sidewinder and an AIM-120 AMRAAM, integrated thrust vectoring nozzles, and maintained control while reaching 60 degrees AOA.

Moreover, during dem/val Boeing provided a 757 as an avionics flying laboratory. Theories were verified and equipment was modified to achieve the

Below: The YF-22's flight test programme was conducted at the Air Force Flight Test Center at Edwards Air Force Base in the Mojave Desert. The prototype is seen flying over one of the base's dry lake beds with a runway clearly marked on the baked clay-like surface. On 25 April, 1992 one of the two prototypes crashed at Edwards, but fortunately no one was injured. Because the programme was so far along, little if any harm was done to the development. Flight testing will resume with the first production prototype F-22 scheduled to roll out of the plant in early 1996.

design goals. The level of stealthiness desired was thought to have been validated by a full-scale radar pole model. Later testing, however, uncovered design flaws that eroded the F-22's low observables characteristics. Design corrections are expected by early 1995 such that no production aircraft will suffer impaired stealthiness. Both Air Force and Lockheed personnel seem relieved that this problem was caught in time to prevent expensive post-production RCS-related modifications from being necesary.

The programme director's only admitted major technical disappointment with the dem/val phase was the inability to use more unconventional material like thermoplastics in the aircraft structure. As it is, the F-22 will be comprised of 26 per cent composites by weight. This results in a sizeable weight reduction when compared to traditional materials. Aluminium will make up only 14 per cent of the F-22 while titanium, with its inherent ballistics resistence qualities, will comprise 30 per cent of the new fighter.

For all its high-tech wizardry, the F-22's design has not inadvertently relegated the pilot to some sort of secondary managerial role. Like most good fighters throughout history, the F-22 with its bubble-type canopy gives the pilot outstanding visibility. The advanced cockpit design reduces workload and offers an environment that maximizes all-important situational awareness.

Being ever more cost conscious, the Air Force, when it initiated the programme for a next generation air superiority fighter, made it clear that it did not want to pay substantially more in comparable-year dollars for the ATF than what it was paying for the F-15. Lockheed estimated the unit flyaway cost for the ATF at $35 million in 1985 dollars. The most recent figure available is $57 million in 1990 dollars.

Plans call for an initial lot of nine F-22s to be built with rollout in early 1996 and flight test starting in mid 1996. The first three aircraft will be used for aerodynamics testing and the remaining six will be used for avionics-related testing. Two static test articles are also scheduled to be built. Production totalling 442 aircraft (down from an earlier level of 648 aircraft) for the Air Force is supposed to begin in 1996 and continue through 2014. First operational readiness is to occur in 2002. Budget pressures may further cut the total Air Force buy and stretch out the delivery schedule. While the Navy has dropped plans for a Naval ATF (NATF), approved foreign buyers could potentially pick up any slack in the production run.

Well into the EMD phase, on 25 April, 1992, the YF-22 prototype powered by Pratt & Whitney YF119 engines entered a pilot-induced oscillation (PIO) mode while in the midst of an attempted afterburner-assisted go-around during a low pass over runway 22 at Edwards Air Force Base. The horizontal stabilisers in concert with the thrust vectoring nozzles alternated wildly starting at only 40 feet above the ground. The oscillating worsened and the aircraft pancaked into the runway with its gear up.

The prototype slid 8,000 feet down the runway before stopping. A fire broke out, but the test pilot emerged from the cockpit unscathed. The aircraft was severely damaged, though still in one piece. Since the Air Force considered that about 75 per cent of the EMD flight test hours already had been accumulated and that over 90 per cent of the test objectives had been met, the decision was made not to repair the crashed prototype nor to resume flight testing with the remaining General Electric YF120-powered prototype. The flight test programme will recommence when the first production prototype rolls out in 1996.

The cause of the crash has been thoroughly studied, and the Air Force is convinced, as evidenced by its investigatory summary, that the aircraft is not inherently flawed. It claims that the aircraft performed as expected given the circumstances. However, reports indicate

Above: The flight test programme's dem/val phase included the inflight launch of the new AIM-120 AMRAAM on 20 December 1990. This test occurred over the range of the Navy's Pacific Missile Test Center, Pt. Mugu, California. It successfully demonstrated missile separation and ignition. The AMRAAM also flew the proper trajectory. The F-22 can carry weaponry internally as a means of minimising its radar cross section (RCS). This capability bodes well for the strike fighter aspect of the F-22. Current plans call for the F-22 in its air superiority configuration to carry an assortment of Sidewinders and AMRAAMs. Also, the F-22 is to be equipped with an M61 20mm Gatling gun.

that software changes may be made to lessen the PIO tendency.

Based on data gathered through late 1991, the F-22 design team froze the aircraft's configuration. The aircraft's length was shortened to 62 feet and 1 inch, and the cockpit moved forward to enhance pilot visibility. Wing span was increased to 44 feet and 6 inches which expanded wing area to 840 square feet. This is expected to improve subsonic cruise efficiency. The sweep of 48 degrees on all leading edge wing and tail surfaces was reduced to 42 degrees to foster better manoeuvrability. Other changes such as reducing the streamlining of the nose will lead to heightened stealthiness.

Owning the skies is a prerequisite to victory in modern warfare. The Persian Gulf War demonstrated the relevance of

air superiority to today's battle-field. Possessing the upper hand with the best air-to-air combat aircraft is now essential to success against a sophisticated enemy.

The nature of the threat to the West has changed with the collapse of the Soviet Union, but widespread instability in the world does pose a series of new dangers. Third World nations have acquired

technologically advanced weapons at an alarming rate. The Commonwealth of Independent States (CIS), succumbing to dire economic circumstances, is selling its military wares to virtually any country paying in hard currency.

So far, eleven nations have purchased the highly capable MiG-29. The Su-27, another very well-regarded Russian fighter, is available for export too. These latest Russian air superiority and counter air fighters are generally considered to be on a par with current generation American fighters — the F-14, F-15, F-16, and F/A-18. In certain respects, the flight performance of the Russian fighters is better. They are, after all, newer designs than their American counterparts. The American fighters do have more impressive avionics, but even this advantage seems to be waning. Training for American air crews is better, giving a qualitative edge.

It is possible that the threat will include modern Western fighters as well. For example, Iraq flew Mirage F-1s against coalition forces in the beginning of 'Operation Desert Storm'. Modification programmes and new designs are under way in various parts of the world.

In the U.S., only one new fighter entered the Air Force inventory in the decade of the 1980s. This was the F-117A, an attack aircraft rather than an air-to-air combat aircraft. Assuming the F-22 begins operational service shortly after the turn of the century, it will have been nearly 30 years since the last air superiority fighter, the F-15, entered the Air Force inventory.

If the U.S. is to retain its technological advantage against probable foes, it has little choice but to proceed in a timely fashion with the F-22 programme. For the only superpower to settle for outdated and outclassed equipment would be a disservice to its military personnel and an unnecessarily hazardous course in an all too often disagreeable world. Budgetary concerns should not delay the Lightning II; it is needed now as was its namesake at another perilous time in history.

Opposite: Northrop, in partnership with McDonnell Douglas, led the competing team in the ATF competition. The Northrop team entry, the YF-23A, was actually the more radical-looking design. It is thought to have been more stealthy, but not as manoeuvrable. In fact, Lockheed has stated that it considered a tail structure with only twin canted vertical surfaces. This reportedly offered superior low observables, but Lockheed ruled out this configuration in favour of a four-surfaced tail configuration which enhances manoeuvrability. Other considerations influencing the Air Force's decision were the apparent lower maintenance costs for the F-22 and the Lockheed team's more accomplished dem/val flight test programme. The Air Force seemed to think the Northrop team's entry was worthy, but riskier than the F-22.

CHAPTER 3
Eurofighter 2000: Design by Committee

Opposite: This artist's impression shows Eurofighter 2000 (then known as the European Fighter Aircraft or EFA) screeching over a cumulus cloud deck towards the top of a loop. Fitted with an array of radar guided and heat-seeking air-to-air missiles, the aircraft is exercising its excellent manoeuvring qualities. Note that the camouflage scheme is low visibility grey.

Below: The first Eurofighter prototype, designated Development Aircraft 1 (DA 1), is at the Manching Flight Test Centre awaiting completion and its first flight.

The story of what is now referred to as Eurofighter 2000 is as much a tale of the trials and triumphs of a delicate alliance among government bureaucracies as it is an account of aeronautical development. The West European consortium for this next generation multi-role fighter was patterned after the successful three-nation Tornado joint venture. However, for Eurofighter 2000, Spain joined the United Kingdom, Germany and Italy to form a four-nation group represented by the NATO European Fighter Aircraft Management Agency (NEFMA).

An industrial partnership called Eurofighter and whose members are British Aerospace, Deutsche Aerospace, Alenia, and Construcciones Aeronauticas is developing the new aircraft. A parallel organization called Eurojet and comprised of Rolls-Royce, Motoren-und Turbinen-Union, Fiat Avio, and Industrie de Turbo Propulsores is responsible for the new engine. These teams have been guided by the European Staff Requirement for Development (ESR-D) which was arrived at by mutual consent of the air forces of the four nations in 1987.

At first known as the European Fighter Aircraft (EFA), this proposed next generation fighter continues to be preceived as the replacement for the four

Left: Engine trials were performed statically on the second Eurofighter 2000 prototype, designated Development Aircraft 2 (DA 2), at the British Aerospace Military Aircraft Division facility at Warton Aerodrome in Lancashire. Engineers watch as the engines are run-up to maximum afterburner on the second day of tests.

nations' aging fleets of Tornados, F-4 Phantoms, F-104 Starfighters, and Mirage F-1s. Purchases of the Rafale or upgraded versions of the F-15, F-16 and F/A-18 were considered but ruled out as not adequate for the future given the sophistication of the potential threat.

The F-22, though viewed as the undisputed superior next generation fighter, was considered too expensive. Another motivating factor in the consortium's pursuing a new fighter is the understandable desire to retain a strong high-tech manufacturing base in each of the constituent countries. Turning to an outside supplier for the weapon system would devastate the defence industries of the four nations and profoundly inhibit their further involvement in complex technical programmes.

Prior to the 1992 Farnborough Air Show, German Defence Minister Volker Ruhe, amid the costly backdrop of a newly-unified Germany, released a political bomb-shell when he announced that his country would withdraw from EFA production because of escalating project costs. He suggested a lighter, less expensive fighter. But the momentum for EFA was strong with first flights in Germany and Britain scheduled for late 1992/early 1993 (since rescheduled for April 1994).

Having come so far on EFA, abandonment was unthinkable to the other consortium members. By December 1992, Germany was persuaded to remain in the programme. In 1995 it will evaluate its participation and decide whether or not to purchase the aircraft.

Below: A full-scale mock-up was pedestal mounted and exhibited publicly at the 1992 Farnborough Air Show. Of course, at that time the future of Eurofighter 2000 was in doubt because of the wavering commitment of the German Defence Minister. Also, at that time, the aircraft was known as the EFA.

Material	Surface Area
CFC	70%
GRP	12%
Metal	15%
Other	3%

- Carbon Fibre Composites
- Aluminium Lithium
- Titanium
- Glass Reinforced Plastic
- Aluminium Casting

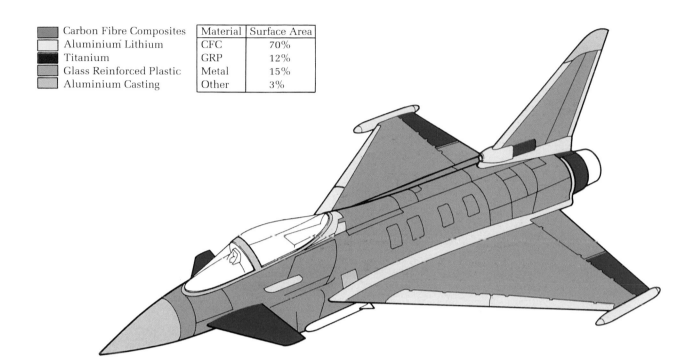

The German view was that EFA's mission requirements had changed since the originally perceived threat of a Soviet-led Warsaw Pact force had essentially disappeared. Accordingly, in the mind of Minister Ruhe, EFA need not be as capable as planned. This sparked controversy since the U.K. took the position that a considerable threat still exists albeit in different form. The end of the Cold War brought its own brand of volatility wherein the bulwark powers of the West would still face sophisticated weapons technology, not the least of which includes upgraded versions of the MiG-29 Fulcrum, notably the MiG-29M, an improved variant of the Su-27 Flanker known as the Su-35 or Super Flanker, and a reported new Russian air superiority fighter dubbed Project 1.42 and possibly carrying the designation MiG-33.

Certain programme requirements may be relaxed, such as the STOL and sustained Mach 2 cruise capabilities. It was decided that partner countries could pick from a menu of options the systems they wish to have equipping the baseline fighter. For example, the less sophisticated avionics option may be selected. Revamped requirements, different workshare arrangements, and outright cost-cutting have resulted in projected savings of up to 30 per cent. In recognition of the changes, EFA was renamed Eurofighter 2000. The team's corporate partners are hoping to gain some profit through sales of the plane to other users.

From the outset of the programme, Eurofighter 2000 was developed as a highly agile, all-weather single-seat fighter, optimized for the air superiority mission, affording each of the partner nations a substantial measure of border defence. At the same time, the aircraft was intended to be adaptable to the air-to-ground strike mission. In fact, it may alternate missions in flight. If the Tornado's history is any guide, there will probably also be ECM and reconnaissance variants.

A range of advanced technologies is being applied to Eurofighter 2000. Eighty-two per cent of the aircraft's skin is either carbon fibre composites or glass reinforced plastic. Construction techniques include superplastic forming and diffusion

Above: Eurofighter 2000 makes extensive use of carbon fibre composites. Incorporation of such materials into the aircraft's structure generally offers strength, durability, a weight savings, and consistently smooth exterior surfaces. This latter contribution enhances low observables as there are fewer imperfections in the aircraft skin that could serve to readily reflect enemy radar waves.

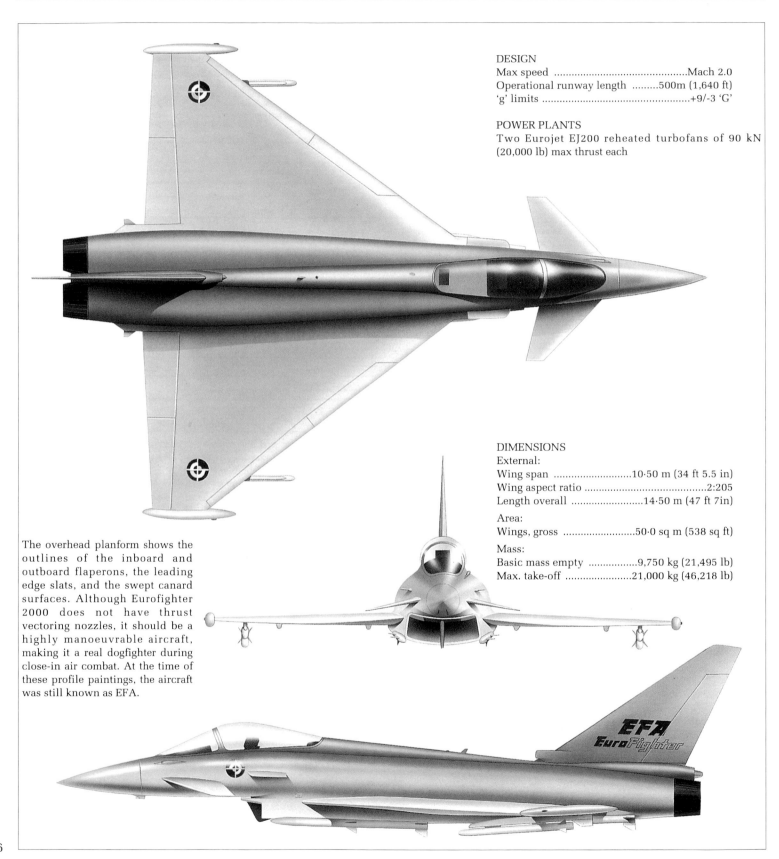

DESIGN
Max speed ....Mach 2.0
Operational runway length ....500m (1,640 ft)
'g' limits ....+9/-3 'G'

POWER PLANTS
Two Eurojet EJ200 reheated turbofans of 90 kN
(20,000 lb) max thrust each

DIMENSIONS
External:
Wing span ....10·50 m (34 ft 5.5 in)
Wing aspect ratio 2:205
Length overall ....14·50 m (47 ft 7in)
Area:
Wings, gross ....50·0 sq m (538 sq ft)
Mass:
Basic mass empty ....9,750 kg (21,495 lb)
Max. take-off ....21,000 kg (46,218 lb)

The overhead planform shows the outlines of the inboard and outboard flaperons, the leading edge slats, and the swept canard surfaces. Although Eurofighter 2000 does not have thrust vectoring nozzles, it should be a highly manoeuvrable aircraft, making it a real dogfighter during close-in air combat. At the time of these profile paintings, the aircraft was still known as EFA.

bonding. The aircraft is controlled by a full-authority digital and quadruplex fly-by-wire system. Sensor fusion will be a feature of the avionics, integrating critical data and displaying them in easily understood and quickly grasped symbology on three multi-function displays (MFDs) to lessen pilot workload and increase situational awareness.

The pilot will wear a helmet with a built-in sight and night vision enhancements. All combat critical data will be displayed on the helmet-mounted sight and a head-up display (HUD). The control stick and throttle lever incorporate more than 20 fingertip functions as part of a hands-on-throttle-and-stick (HOTAS) design.

Like the other West European future fighter designs that have emerged in recent years, Eurofighter 2000 is a delta/canard. Each wing trailing edge has one inboard and one outboard flaperon. Each wing leading edge has two slats that combined are nearly full-span. These slats automatically provide optimal camber at all angles of attack (AOA). The rudder is attached to the vertical stabilizer. Ensuring recovery from high AOA manoeuvres, there are all-moving canard surfaces below the forward section of the canopy.

Eurofighter 2000 designers boast that the aircraft is stealthy. While ground tests reportedly show that the airframe has a low radar cross section (RCS), the problem the Eurofighter 2000 has with low observables stems in large part from the fact that with the exception of its 27mm cannon all weapons are carried externally. Four of the fuselage stores stations are semi-recessed to reduce the RCS and to provide a degree of aerodynamic streamlining. But there are nine additional stores stations, three of which can accommodate external fuel tanks.

These protuberances will tend to counteract the aircraft's stealthiness. Early studies conducted by the consortium suggested, however, that Eurofighter 2000 would outperform any known Russian fighter and any known or postulated Western fighter except the F-22 in beyond visual range (BVR) combat.

The aircraft's self-protection equipment includes the Defensive Aids Sub-System (DASS). For economic reasons this system may not be included in the German and Spanish production models. The DASS system is carried internally and is integrated with the aircraft's avionics. It will detect enemy threats within a wide radius using antennas located in various parts of the fuselage and wings. It will also have an ECM capability allowing it to jam enemy radars. Equipment includes chaff/flare dispensers.

Offensively, Eurofighter 2000 will be able to acquire targets way beyond visual range with its advanced ECR 90 multi mode pulse Doppler radar. This system can track up to eight targets at once. In addition, for closer range air combat and for air-to-ground missions, there is an infrared search and track (IRST) system. The sensor of the internally-carried dual-mode forward-looking infrared (FLIR) system is noticeable as a bulge on the port forward fuselage. First generation FLIRs were carried as external pods.

Power will come from two Eurojet EJ 200 afterburning engines. Each can produce up to 20,000 lbs of thrust. Designed for growth, a 15 per cent increase in thrust may be possible. Construction is fully modular which facilitates maintenance. The engines have a full authority digital engine control (FADEC) system.

The EJ 200 incorporates modern technology in the form of blisks, powder metals, and single crystal materials. Life cycle costs are projected at 40 per cent less than an equivalent engine in operation today. Because of the expected reliability rates, the EJ 200 will probably have wide applicability to single-engined aircraft, and in a non-afterburning (dry) version would be appropriate for trainer/light attack aircraft.

Designers at British Aerospace had the foresight to field a technology demonstrator. Called the Experimental Aircraft Programme (EAP), construction of the aircraft began in summer 1984. First flight occurred in August 1986, and flight testing continued through May 1991.

During this time, a total of 259 flights were made. Basic design features such as the air brake were validated. Progress was made towards the flight control system. Experience was gained in the use of new materials like carbon fibre composites. The design of the production prototypes is remarkably similar to the general outlines of the EAP. The five years of demonstrator flight testing succeeded in reducing programme risks.

The major NATO countries are in need of an advanced multi-role fighter. Their inventories are currently occupied by fighters that will not be adequate for the threats of the early 21st century. Some, like the F-104, are already obsolete. Eurofighter 2000 is an answer to the requirement.

Although, like its West European counterparts the Rafale and the Gripen, Eurofighter 2000 does not represent a radical leap forward, it promises to add meaningful new capability. If there are no more politically induced reversals, Eurofighter 2000 could enter service shortly after the turn of the century.

In the meantime, the consortium's member nations are addressing their pressing air defence requirements. For example, Italy has agreed to a ten-year lease of 24 Tornado F-3s from Britain's Royal Air Force. Italy is also taking the extraordinary step of extending the service life of its license-built F-104S fighters through an extensive upgrade programme.

Opposite: From August 1986 to May 1991, a demonstrator called the Experimental Aircraft Programme (EAP) was flight tested by British Aerospace as a prelude to the final design, manufacture, and flight testing of Eurofighter 2000 prototypes. The success of the EAP contributed greatly to the overall programme. The prototypes are remarkably similar in appearance to the demonstrator, which suggests that the early design concept for this next generation fighter was valid.

CHAPTER 4
Rafale: Sculpturesque Fighter

Below: An impressive array of Rafales is displayed by Dassault Aviation. In the foreground is Rafale M 01, the first pre-production prototype for the Aéronavale. Note the launch tow bar of the nose gear. The French Navy is preparing to alter its carrier catapult launch systems to more closely resemble the systems in place on U.S. aircraft carriers. In the middle is Rafale C 01, the first pre-production prototype for the Armée de l'Air. Its all black paint scheme suggests night missions to optimise stealth. In the background is the Rafale A, a flying technology demonstrator that paved the way for the future French fighter. It was a remarkably successful proof-of-concept aircraft.

For more than three decades, France's Dassault Aviation has been the world's leading proponent and manufacturer of partially tail-less, delta-winged fighters. These distinctive design features, embodied in the famous Mirage pedigree, yielded not only a sleek appearance but impressive speed performance.

Dassault's next generation fighter, the Rafale, is a particularly aesthetic delta design with, for the first time in the French fighter line, moveable foreplanes. (In the mid 1970s, the Israelis built the Kfir, a fighter patterned after the Mirage V and which was modified with fixed foreplanes.) The first Rafale pre-production prototypes are undergoing a rigorous and ambitious flight test programme as this book goes to press. Three variants are scheduled to be produced:

1. the ACT (Avion de Combat Tactique) for the Armée de l'Air, the French Air Force, designated the C model;

2. the B model, which is a two-seat variant for training, but which will be fully combat capable; and,

3. the ACM (Avion de Combat Marin) for the Aéronautique Navale, the French navy's air arm, designated the M model.

The design is based on a technology demonstrator, designated the Rafale A, which first flew in July 1986. This proof-of-concept aircraft contributed a great deal to the programme's developmental success. Critical design elements were able to be refined in the pre-production phase because of knowledge gained in the Rafale A's extensive flight testing.

In accord with accepted doctrine that calls for a single airframe type to perform

many missions, the production Rafale will be expected to assume a multitude of roles. The Rafale is perceived, first, as an air superiority fighter. It is also designed for ground attack, including a nuclear strike capability. The Rafale will be adaptable to a range of related electronic warfare, defence suppression, and recce missions. As one of the world's few remaining militaries with full-fledged, catapult-equipped aircraft carriers, the navalized Rafale will come none too soon as a carrier-based replacement for aging aircraft in the Aéronavale's inventory.

The fuselage in sculpted with recesses in the area under the cockpit just forward of the engines' semi-ventral air inlets. Aft of the main portion of the cockpit, and set

somewhat low so as not to interfere with pilot visibility, are the moveable foreplanes, or canards. These active control surfaces on the Rafale C 01, the first pre-production aircraft, are proportionally larger than those on the demonstrator. These canards provide for even greater manoeuvrability and are most welcome on the Rafale M since controllability at slow speeds for landing approaches to carrier decks is critical.

Power is provided by two Snecma M88-2 engines, specially developed for this fighter and each capable of 17,000 lb maximum thrust. From this advanced baseline engine, derivatives may follow that, according studies, could boost maximum thrust to levels of 21,000 to 23,000 lb.

Above: The Rafale C 01 is an uncommonly sleek and highly-sculpted aircraft. This angle affords an excellent view of its movable canards, which add considerably to manoeuvrability, a key attribute for a fighter. This pre-production prototype already is emblazoned with the red, white and blue roundels of the Armee de l'Air, the French Air Force.

As of this writing, a total of 23 of the M88-2 engines have been produced. So far inflight testing has gone exceptionally well. The Rafale C 01 flew supersonic on its very first flight on 19 May 1991. It did so without use of afterburners. Moreover, the aircraft took off in only about 400 metres. Less than a month later it offered a display of its superb handling qualities at the opening of the Paris Air Show.

Notable technological advances in the M88-2 engine are single-crystal cooled turbine blades and powder metallurgy which increases tolerance to high temperatures. The engine's design is modular for ease of maintenance. Also, the M88-2 uses a full authority digital control system that has built-in redundancy. The engine has gone from idle to maximum thrust with afterburner in just three seconds, an impressive performance that is necessary for the powerplants of the carrier-based variant.

Dassault, for security reasons, has remained understandably tight-lipped about the details of its cockpit

Right: Carrier suitability tests of the Rafale M 01 were initiated in summer 1992 at the U.S. Navy's facilities in Lakehurst, New Jersey and Patuxent River, Maryland. Only the U.S. has the resources to conduct full scale trials on shore for the catapult launch systems planned for the Rafale. Arrested landing tests on lengthy runways at these facilities were also performed. Early results are promising.

instrumentation. It is known that included are a wide-field holographic head-up display, a head-level display for presentation of the tactical situation, and two side-by-side head-down displays for presentation of aircraft system status reports in colour imagery as well as mission data.

The Rafale's pilot will benefit from a newly-developed display-in-visor helmet. Essential aircraft and weapons data can be projected onto the visor so that the pilot does not lose sight of this vital symbology

regardless of the direction in which he turns. Called OPIS (operational sight integrated system), it will permit target acquisition/designation. With built-in electronics and oxygen mask the helmet weighs 3.19 lb. This arrangement may constitute a bit of a weight penalty and some inconvenience in terms of mask adjustment.

The pilot's seat is reclined 29 degrees to lessen the vertical distance between the pilot's heart and brain to improve resistance to G loads. Initially, the pilot's seat was angled back 31 degrees, but this was found to be too extreme in that shorter pilots would have trouble reaching the keyboards. With his hand on the control stick, the pilot will have fingertip access to many systems. The stick has numerous controls built into it as part of the HOTAS (hands on throttle and stick) system.

Operational Rafales will be outfitted with a sophisticated electronic countermeasures system known as SPECTRA (systéme de protection et d'évitement des conduites de tir du Rafale). Based on the earlier ICMS (integrated countermeasures system) which was successfully tested on a Mirage 2000, the new ECM system will be divided into ten constituent parts, each located separately within the aircraft.

SPECTRA will be integrated with navigation and weapons systems to easily provide the Rafale's pilot with an overview of his aircraft's status in the context of its immediate environment. This will enhance

Above: The first pre-production prototype of the navalised Rafale variant is shown over calm seas in formation with an Aéronavale Super Etendard, which it will replace. Low visibility grey is the preferred camouflage paint scheme for the Rafales in Aéronavale service. Note the electronics pod built into the Rafale's fin.

43

the pilot's situational awareness. Onboard computers and a dedicated data bus will speedily process and transmit the incoming data from SPECTRA sensors.

A first for Europe is the development for Rafale of an electronic scanning radar by France's Thomson-CSF. The new RBE2 radar has been tested aboard a specially modified Dassault Falcon 20 corporate jet. When perfected, the radar will be able to track several aerial targets at once and also provide for low-level terrain following when flying in the air-to-ground mode. The Rafale will also have an infrared search and track (IRST) system.

Dassault has played up the Rafale's stealthiness. Indeed, the aircraft is petite (the Rafale A demonstrator was a little larger) and it is shaped to reduce the radar cross section. However, operational Rafales will have 14 external stores stations (13 for the navalized version) which will be able to accommodate up to eight tons of external stores, everything from bombs, missiles, fuel tanks, to electronics pods.

Clearly, to retain a modicum of stealth, the Rafale would have to fly relatively lightly armed. Wisely, its designers have mounted internally the GIAT Industries DEFA 791 fast-firing 30mm cannon. This weapon should be able to penetrate most armour during close-in fights.

The first carrier suitability tests for the navalized version were conducted in the U.S. during 1992 and will continue on and off through 1994. Catapult launch and arrested landing tests were conducted at the Naval Air Warfare Center in Lakehurst, New Jersey. Later, a series of arrested landings were made at the Naval Air Test Center at Patuxent River, Maryland. The test article was the Rafale M 01, Dassault's first pre-production variant for the Aéronavale.

The first set of tests was successful. Testing had to be conducted in the U.S. since it is the only Western nation with the facilities for the elaborate testing required.

France has only two aircraft carriers accommodating fixed wing aircraft — the *Clemenceau* and the *Foch*. These carriers now use a relatively small British catapult system. In 1998, a new and larger carrier is scheduled to enter service with the French Navy. This carrier, the *Charles de Gaulle*, has been designed on the principles applied to U.S. Navy carriers. The *Charles de Gaulle* will have a catapult system like that on current U.S. supercarriers. The *Foch* will be retrofitted with a catapult system akin to the American system; however, because of a shorter deck the ship will have to use a 'ski jump' to launch the Rafale Ms.

As is always the case when a fixed wing aircraft goes from being ground-based to carrier-based, there is an immediate weight penalty because of the beefed-up landing gear, launch tow bar, arrester hook, reinforced structure, and in the case of the Rafale M the addition of a folding built-in ladder to minimize flight deck clutter. Dassault claims that the overall weight increase of the Rafale M over the Rafale C is only eight per cent. There are no plans for a folding wing. Apparently, the aircraft's small size will suffice for stowage purposes.

In many respects the Rafale development programme has been a showcase. Not aligned with any co-equal airframe manufacturers in the development or production, Dassault has been the sole overseer — the boss where the buck stops. The company devised a configuration for its country's next generation fighter, believed in it, and proceeded to build a technology demonstrator and fly it to validate the concept.

With a commendable single-mindedness, the company has succeeded in a timely manner in developing an advanced fighter for the future that promises to contribute positively to the fine reputation of Dassault's past and current fighters. If the momentum continues uninterrupted, first deliveries of the production Rafales to the French Air Force and Navy will occur in late 1996, well before the West European consortium and the American joint venture deliver their next generation fighters. The Rafale is also shaping up as a formidable competitor in the international marketplace which Dassault has already cultivated.

CHAPTER 5
Gripen: Lightweight and Adaptable

Below: A graceful-looking fighter, the JAS 39 is highly man-oeuvrable. The aircraft's light weight and moving canards contribute to its agility. These highly-desirable attributes for close-in air fighting are partially diminished by the restricted rearward visibility. The single-engine configuration is a trade-off. It does not offer the same protection as a twin-engine configuration, but it is obviously less expensive in terms of upfront and life cycle costs.

The Swedish Air Force, looking for a replacement for its aged fleet of Draken and Viggen fighters, has turned to the JAS consortium. The acronym JAS is derived from the three essential missions of the new fighter: air defence, attack, and reconnaissance (Jakt, Attack and Spaning). The four companies comprising the core of the JAS consortium are Saab-Scania (aircraft development), Volvo Flygmotor (engine), Ericsson Radar Electronics (radar, computers and displays), and FFV Aerotech (test and maintenance equipment).

After a ten-year development effort, including an intensive flight test programme, the first production aircraft, No. 101, made its initial flight in September 1992. Known as the JAS 39 Gripen, the new all-weather fighter entered operational service with the Swedish Air Force in June 1993. Under the first contract, five prototypes and 30 production aircraft are to be delivered. A contract signed in June 1992 calls for an additional 110 Gripens to be delivered through the year 2001. If budget permits, a total of 16 Swedish Air Force squadrons

may be equipped with the Gripen, bringing total domestic deliveries of the aircraft to about 300.

Perhaps more than any of the other next generation Western fighters, the Gripen's design has been driven by cost considerations. While it shares a canard/delta configuration with the fighter designs of other West European nations, it is dissimilarly a single-engine aircraft. The absence of a second engine reduces upfront costs as well as operational costs.

Because of its single-engine design, the Gripen is comparatively lighter. In fact, through application of carbon fibre composites throughout approximately 30 per cent of the airframe, the use of a fly-by-wire flight control system, down-scaling, and other innovations, the Gripen is actually smaller in physical dimension and only about half the weight (nearly 18,000 lb at take-off) of its immediate predecessor, the Saab Viggen. At the same time, technological advances allow the Gripen to

Above: One of the prototype Gripens parked on a ramp has an assortment of possible weapons including infrared- and radar-guided missiles arrayed around it. In front is an ammunition belt to feed the aircraft's port side 27mm Mauser high velocity gun. The Gripen was designed to be equally adept at air-to-air and air-to-ground combat.

Opposite: The Gripen will replace the Saab Draken and evenually the Saab Viggen in the Swedish Air Force. Since resources are scarce, this next generation fighter must have the adaptability to execute the diverse missions of air defence, ground and sea attack, and reconnaissance. State-of-the-art electronics allow the pilot to switch the aircraft's mission orientation with a push of the button.

carry the same weapons load, exercise greater manoeuvrability, perform better in combat across the spectrum of foreseeable missions, and cost less to operate.

A linchpin in the success of the Gripen is its powerplant. The RM 12 afterburning turbofan is derived from the well-regarded General Electric F404-GE-400 engine which has been in use for over a decade. Under a teaming arrangement, 60 per cent of each engine is provided by General Electric and the remaining 40 per cent is the responsibility of Volvo Flygmotor which performs final assembly at its Trollhättan factory.

Thrust of the RM 12 engine has been increased by approximately 10 per cent over the General Electric baseline engine thrust to a maximum level of about 17,800 lb. This improvement has resulted from an increase in the turbine inlet temperature and the airflow into the fan. There have been some changes in hot section materials to accommodate the higher temperature and pressure levels. Further thrust enhancements are possible. Both the inlet area and the fan have been reinforced to protect against the possibility of bird strikes on low-level missions over ground and over sea.

As the Gripen has but one engine, reliability is absolutely imperative. The F404 was chosen as the starting point for the Gripen's powerplant in large measure because of its exemplary operational history. Other factors influencing this decision included the General Electric engine's compactness, high thrust-to-weight ratio, and relative fuel efficiency. Moreover, the engine's successful market penetration and widespread use assures continued product support, an important consideration for prospective Gripen export sales.

Cockpit instrumentation is dominated by three electronic head-down displays (HDDs) and one wide-angle (28 degrees by 22 degrees field of view) holographic head-up display (HUD). While the HDDs are interchangeable, they are each generally dedicated to providing readouts of flight data, sensor data, and the tactical situation,

respectively. These displays are augmented by a few "standby" instruments in traditional dial and gauge format. Between the HUD and the middle HDD is the main mode selector. System integration allows for this uncluttered and pilot-friendly arrangement.

The idea of a sidestick was rejected in favour of a control stick located in the centre. The centre location was determined to be the more practical placement since in the heat of combat the pilot's right hand or arm might become disabled, requiring the use of his left hand on the grip.

The only apparent deficiency in cockpit design is the razorback canopy that restricts the pilot's view. It is surprising that this aircraft that will not enjoy all the advantages of the most expensive and sophisticated next generation fighters and that, therefore, will be more likely to fight close-in air-to-air engagements does not have a bubble style canopy giving the pilot an opportunity to check his six o'clock position.

The Gripen has been designed for almost instantaneous transition from one mission to the other. By the press of a button, the pilot can transform the aircraft from, for example, the air-to-ground combat mode to the air-to-air combat mode. The avionics software systems integration allows this rapid switch and makes the Gripen a true multi-role fighter. Of course, to be effective in dual missions in a single flight, the aircraft must be outfitted before take-off with the ordnance appropriate for those missions.

The Gripen is an inherently unstable aircraft and is critically reliant on its full-authority triplex digital electronic flight control system. Flight manoeuvres that would lead to catastrophic consequences are automatically limited. The Gripen has about 40 computers on board. Most of these are linked together in a web through three redundant 1553B data buses.

When discussing the Ericsson PS-05/A pulse Doppler radar, JAS consortium officials point out that the Gripen's name is based on the eagle-headed griffin of mythology. The PS-05/A radar is, in their

dramatic metaphor, the "eagle eyes" of the aircraft.

The radar was built by Ericsson expressly for the Gripen. It has multiple-target track-while-scan capability as well as look-down capability. Even when beyond visual range (BVR), the Gripen's pilot can launch several radar-guided missiles simultaneously at different aerial targets. A decision should be forthcoming as to which radar-guided missile – AMRAAM, Active Sky Flash or MICA – will equip the Gripen.

Mounted in the nose, the powerful radar has a mechanically-scanned planar array antenna. Modular in design, the radar lends itself to maintainability.

Detailed flight performance data have not been widely disseminated, but it is known that the Gripen can travel at supersonic speeds at any altitude up to its service ceiling. In the flight test programme, it has taken off with a considerable load and climbed to a high cruise altitude without using its afterburner. Its closely-coupled, fully-moving canard gives added controllability at low speeds when landing and at high angles of attack when dogfighting. For close-in air-to-air combat, the Gripen's pilot has the

Right: The Volvo Flygmotor's RM 12 afterburning turbofan, derived from the General Electric F404-GE-400, can produce up to 17,800 lb of thrust and give the lightweight JAS 39 Gripen rocket-like performance on take-off. Conversely, when landing, the Gripen can fit onto short fields in part because its moving canards are pointed down during roll-out and serve as big air brakes. These STOL capabilities are important since Swedish military doctrine calls for the dispersal of fighter aircraft to austere fields and roadways in wartime.

option of a port-side 27mm Mauser high velocity gun.

The Swedish Air Force believes it is essential to the nation's defence that its air assets be deployable to numerous remote areas. By dispersing the fighter force throughout the country in time of national emergency, a tactical advantage would be gained. In fact, a plan exists to use parts of the nation's highway system as runways for operational Gripens.

Contributing to this deployment capability is the Gripen's reputed STOL porformance. The Gripen's canards can serve as huge air brakes to shorten the landing roll. The aircraft's simplicity and ease of maintenance also help to make this kind of fielding possible. The Swedish Air Force contends that minimally skilled ground crews can service this fleet of fighters at scattered makeshift facilities. A built-in auxiliary power unit (APU) obviates the need for external APUs and makes start-up a logistically uncomplicated affair.

In the event of air attack, Swedish military planners believe that runway denial would be among the enemy's main priorities. Badly cratered runways would be unusable. The alternative is the

country's roads network. As part of its training, the Swedish Air Force has actually moved some of its earlier generation fighters to roadways for a real world feel of what it would be like in wartime. Even in these austere surroundings, the Gripen is expected to generate a high sortie rate.

The Gripen's flight test programme has not been without incident. The first prototype was destroyed in a landing accident in February 1989 after only six flights. Cause of the crash was faulty onboard software in the electronic flight control system. Irretrievable pilot-induced oscillation (PIO) occurred. Fortunately, the test pilot, Lars Radestrom, survived and rejoined the flight test programme which resumed and picked up momentum. The software deficiency was believed to have been rectified along with some powerplant flaws.

Flight testing proceeded well with design goals being met or exceeded. The test pilots reported that the Gripen demonstrated excellent handling characteristics.

However, on 8 August 1993, production aircraft No.102, the first delivered to the Swedish Air Force, crashed while performing during Stockholm's annual water festival. While being abruptly manoeuvered, the Gripen went into an unrecoverable stall. Again Lars Radestrom was at the controls and again he ejected safely. Although the aircraft was destroyed, no one was injured. Like the earlier crash, the cause was traced to the software. It was believed that rectification of the latest quirk could be accomplished with relative ease.

A JAS 39B two-seat tactical trainer is being developed. Fourteen of these will be delivered to the Swedish Air Force with first flight planned for 1996.

Anxious to profit from the development of its new fighter, the JAS consortium is aggressively marketing the Gripen for export. Interestingly, it has been learned that British Aerospace is exploring the possibility of joining the Gripen programme as an international marketer of the aircraft since the fighter potentially fills the mid-level void in the company's current and projected fighter product line.

In many respects the Gripen is like the F-16: single-engined, lightweight, highly manoeuvrable, multi-role, easily maintained, flown by one pilot, and relatively low upfront and life cycle costs. The Gripen may find a niche among financially strapped governments interested in a brand new airframe design and modern cockpit instrumentation.

The Gripen's successful development, especially in the face of potentially devastating flight accidents, is a credit to Sweden's technological infrastructure. For a country the size of Sweden to have produced a next generation fighter virtually on its own is a major accomplishment. In recognition of the enormous capital infusion and the far-flung technical expertise required for the development of new, competitive combat aircraft, it is likely that the Gripen's replacement years from now will be the product of a joint venture involving the aerospace industries of other countries.

Opposite: Gripens are being assembled by the Saab Military Aircraft Division of Saab-Scania in Linkoping, Sweden. A total of 140 Gripens have been contracted for through the year 2001. Approximately another 160 are anticipated for the Swedish Air Force, which perceives the Gripen as the backbone of its operations for up to the next 40 years. There are hopes that this indigenous Swedish multirole fighter will be acquired by other nations.

CHAPTER 6
FS-X: Falcon Clone

Below: Prime contractor, Mitsubishi, unveiled a full-scale FS-X mockup in 1992. It was studied, resulting in 300 recommended improvements. Construction of the first flight test prototype began in mid-1993. First flight is scheduled to occur in mid-1995. Plans call for the FS-X to replace the Mitsubishi F-1 currently in service.

In the mid-1980s, the Japan Defense Agency envisioned a brand-new homegrown twin-engined fighter taking over the air defence mission served by the Mitsubishi Heavy Industries F-1. But politics interceded and the decision was made to jointly develop the replacement aircraft with the U.S., using the venerable General Dynamics (now Lockheed) F-16 Fighting Falcon as the baseline.

The Japanese Air Self-Defense Force has special requirements in that patrol missions are long-range, given the extent of the island country's surrounding airspace and that much of the flying is over water. To the discomfort of some, reportedly including even pilots of the Japanese Air

Self-Defense Force, the selected replacement aircraft has only one engine. For extended over-water operations, pilots generally like the redundancy offered by two or more engines.

In view of mission requirements, the FS-X is larger than the F-16. Specifically, the FS-X's fuselage is about one metre longer and its wing span is also about one metre longer, giving the FS-X 25 per cent more wing area. Mitsubishi is the programme's prime contractor.

As a co-development project, a 40 per cent workshare was negotiated for General Dynamics, the lead U.S. participant. Also, a two-way technology transfer arrangement between the U.S. and Japan was

established. From the outset, there were dire predictions that this joint fighter programme would enable the Japanese to develop a competitive indigenous commercial and military aircraft manufacturing industry. It was felt that as Japan had become a world force in automobiles and consumer electronics, so it might in aerospace.

In response to the warning cries, General Dynamics was prohibited from providing the source codes for the F-16's fly-by-wire (FBW) flight control system. This setback combined with the technical hurdles associated with the major redesign of the F-16 have pushed the FS-X programme a couple of years behind schedule. The earliest an FS-X squadron could be operational is about the turn of the century.

It should be pointed out that Mitsubishi equipped a T-2 testbed with a FBW flight control system in what it called its control configured vehicles (CCV) research programme. This unique T-2 was flight tested from 1983 to 1986. It is believed that the data ascertained from the CCV effort will allow the Japanese to develop the source codes for the FS-X. There was a six month interruption in the source codes development because Japan Aviation Electronics, the principal developer, had been suspended from involvement for illegal exports it made to Iran.

The FS-X's nose will be reshaped and elongated to accommodate a new indigenously-developed active-phased array radar. Power will come from the General Electric F110-GE-129 Increased Performance Engine (IPE) built under licence. This engine is derived from the proven and successful F110-GE-100. The new engine is in the 29,000 lb thrust class. The engine's full-authority digital electronic control (FADEC) system reduces total parts count, provides redundancy for safety, and offers greater reliability. Recent model F-16C/Ds use this advanced engine.

The joint development calls for Lockheed to manufacture the FS-X's wing using a cocuring process pioneered in Japan dating from the early 1980s. With cocuring the components that comprise a structure are cured and bonded together as one piece. Lockheed Fort Worth Company has successfully produced an integral wing fuel tank using the cocuring process. The FS-X's wing box and wing lower skin will be cocured structures.

Cocured structures have the advantage of reducing weight. Once tooling is verified, the process is less complex than conventional manufacturing techniques and involves the use of fewer fasteners. Lockheed may be able to apply its newly-acquired cocuring knowledge to upgrades of existing aircraft and to new designs, especially in regard to wing structures.

In May 1992, the Japan Defense Agency's Technical Research and Development Institute reviewed a full-scale wooden mock-up of the FS-X. More than 300 minor improvements were suggested in the resulting TRDI report. These recommendations will be incorporated in the final design.

Construction of the first FS-X flight test prototype began in the second quarter of 1993 with first flight planned for the third quarter of 1995. The project's test schedule calls for four flying prototypes and two static-test articles. Within a year or so following initial flight tests, a production decision will be made.

If production is begun, a total of about 130 FS-Xs could be acquired for the Japanese Air Self-Defense Force. The fighters would most probably be employed in the intercept, close air support, and anti-shipping missions. They would complement the F-15Js that are licence-built by Mitsubishi. In fact, FS-X production would likely occur at Mitsubishi's Nagoya plant where F-15J production will soon be winding down.

The real benefit of the FS-X programme to the Japanese aerospace industry may very well be not the fighter scheduled to enter operational service early in the next century, but the creation of a technology base that opens the way for fuller involvement in the world aerospace marketplace. Global competitive pressures will probably intensify with free market philosophies dominating many previously state-controlled economies. Under such circumstances, Japanese aerospace companies, rather than go it alone, may link in an expanding series of alliances with overseas competitors that possess the lead in critical technologies.

If nothing else, Japanese industry has learned from the FS-X experience that the development of a highly sophisticated combat aircraft, even if patterned after a proven design, is fraught with hazards. The timetable delays and cost overruns of the FS-X programme are reminders of the risks involved when ambitions run high.

Opposite: The FS-X's kinship to the Lockheed F-16 Fighting Falcon is clearly evident in this artist's rendering. Major design changes from the F-16 include a larger wing (made in an advanced cocuring process), an elongated fuselage, an indigenously developed digital electronic flight control system, and a re-configured nose to accommodate a Japanese active-phased array radar. The two Japanese Air Self-Defense Force fighters depicted here are carrying external fuel tanks to extend their range, presumably in connection with the expected missions of intercept, close air support, and anti-shipping. Great distances are involved in patroling for the island nation, so aircraft range is an especially important design consideration.

CHAPTER 7
Ching-Kuo: Indigenous Defensive Fighter

In response to the 1982 American embargo of General Dynamics (now Lockheed) F-16s and Northrop F-20s directed against the Republic of China (Taiwan), the government-owned and military-controlled Aero Industry Development Center (AIDC) embarked on a programme to design and produce a native fighter. The deteriorating condition of the F-104 Starfighters and the older technology of the F-5 Freedom Fighters in the inventory of the Republic of China Air Force (RoCAF) have made fighter replacement a prime Taiwanese objective. General Dynamics was engaged as a consultant on the development of this replacement aircraft, the Indigenous Defensive Fighter (IDF), also known as the Ching-Kuo.

The F-16's influence is conspicuous starting with the sleek planform all the way to the pilot's right-hand sidestick and 30 degree reclined seat. The cockpit instrumentation is anchored with a centre console that has conventional dials and gauges, sided by monochrome multi-function displays (MFDs). There is also a head-up display (HUD). Plans call for block change upgrades of the avionics package since it is based on the avionics developed for the ill-fated F-20.

The IDF has a Lear Astronics digital fly-by-wire flight control system. Its multi-mode pulse Doppler radar, based on the GE Aerospace APG-67 and known as the Golden Dragon 53, is highly capable.

The most obvious departure from the F-16's design is the incorporation of two engines. An engine joint venture started in 1982 and known as International Turbine Engine Corporation (ITEC) combined the resources of the Garrett Engine Division of Allied Signal and AIDC. The resulting powerplant is the F125/TFE1042-70, which provides maximum augmented thrust of 9,460 lb.

Taiwanese programme managers now believe that this level of engine thrust is inadequate given the current threat posed by mainland China which employs sophisticated Sukhoi Su-27 Flankers. A higher thrust engine in the 12,500 lb class is desired. Later model IDFs would have such higher thrust engines installed while earlier production models might be retro-fitted.

This new requirement touched off a competition between ITEC and General Electric. ITEC proposed an improved performance engine, designated the F125X. General Electric, on the other hand, offered the J101/SF, a scaled-down derivative of its F404 engine that has accumulated in excess of three million flight hours. In light of changing circumstances, however, the thrust enhancement effort was shelved.

The continuing flight test programme has been marred by mishaps. In October 1989, five months after the prototype's first flight, the aircraft's nosewheel collapsed. In July the following year a fatal crash of the second prototype occurred. Although the wreckage was not recoverable from the Taiwan Strait, it is believed that there was a flutter-induced structural failure of the all-moving tailplanes. Consequently, the metal control surfaces will be replaced with structures made of composites.

These drawbacks have not severely hindered the IDF programme. Indeed, in 1992 the first of ten pre-production models,

Below: The first pre-production model of Taiwan's Indigenous Defensive Fighter (IDF), also known as the Ching-Kuo, made its first flight in early 1992. It is a two-seat trainer version of the twin-engine fighter. Design and production consultant on the project has been General Dynamics (now Lockheed). Not surprisingly, the IDF in many respects resembles the Lockheed F-16 Fighting Falcon.

a two-seat version, was successfully flown. The IDF, in fact, appears to be a very agile fighter with a top speed of about Mach 2. It also seems capable of fulfilling the air defence, ground attack, and reconnaissance roles. The twin-engine configuration affords the reliability sought for the island nation's extended over-water requirements.

Yet, politics have a strange way of sometimes intervening in military programmes. Shortly before the 1992 U.S. presidential election, the policy to restrict sales of advanced weapons to Taiwan, apparently as a means of placating mainland China, was reversed and President Bush, trailing in the polls and trying to improve the domestic unemployment situation, announced the authorization of the sale of 150 F-16s to Taiwan. Soon afterwards, the French government announced a plan to sell up to 100 Mirage 2000s to Taiwan.

These foreign fighter purchases by Taiwan may have been motivated by the need to fill a perceived gap that will exist between the phase-out of aging aircraft and the operational deployment of the IDF. There is also the financial issue — how can Taiwan afford all of these top-notch Western fighters and at the same time produce a sizable quantity of its own fighters? Originally, a total buy of about 250 IDFs was envisioned. In 1993, planned production was cut to 130, and there is speculation that only the first block of 60 will be built.

Despite Taiwan's last-minute decision to substantially fall back on off-the-shelf Western fighters, the IDF programme represents an impressive step. Whether or not the new fighter goes into production, its development shows how even a small nation can achieve some technologically gratifying results.

The world's established aerospace businesses would be wise to recognize the potential of emerging technical enterprises, particularly in the Pacific Rim, that have an educated staff, an eager labour force, and boundless determination. These fundamentals can make for a fierce competitor or a golden partner.

Below: Several IDF prototypes have been extensively flight tested. Each has nearly 300 real-time telemetry relay channels for instantaneous review of key flight performance data. Like the F-16, the pilot's seat is angled back to lessen the vertical distance between heart and brain as a means of improving G-load tolerance. Also, as in the F-16, there is a right-hand sidestick. This prototype is in a multicoloured flight test paint scheme.

CHAPTER 8
X-31: Post-Stall Manoeuvrability

The fundamentals of close-in air-to-air combat have changed little since the time of the Red Baron. Manoeuvring for advantageous scoring position is still part of the fighter pilot's repertoire. It is true that with the onset of the missile age, a belief arose that World War I-style dogfights would be a thing of the past. The new theory held that air-to-air missiles, with presumed pinpoint accuracy and beyond visual range (BVR) capability, would permanently retire the kind of air fighting immortalized by the legendary aces. Some even speculated on the replacement of pilots with robots.

Disastrous American kill/loss ratios in the Vietnam air war proved that the new theory on aerial combat was at least premature. The U.S. military instituted corrective programmes, notably the Navy's Top Gun training that re-educated fighter pilots in the art of air combat manoeuvring. Results improved dramatically thereafter.

The longstanding predictions of electronic omnipotence in air warfare did come closer to fruition in more recent conflicts like the Bekaa Valley incident in 1982 and the air campaign of the Persian Gulf War in 1991. At long last, the radar-guided missile, so promising on paper and in tests but so dismal in real world experience, reached a level of lethal refinement.

During the Vietnam War, U.S. fighter pilots would not untypically fire a radar-guided missile at long range first only to have it miss, necessitating the launch of a heat-seeker at close range. The more likely scenario these days is reflected in the preponderance of AEW (airborne early warning) assets directing fighters to the vicinity of tracked aerial targets. Once in the ballpark but while still too distant to be seen, the fighters can lock-on and score with BVR missiles like the new AIM-120 AMRAAM (advanced medium range air-to-air missile).

Of course, the electronic screen is not invincible. An equally sophisticated foe might be able to crack through it. In that case, the air battle reverts to the old-fashioned dogfight, referred to in fighter pilot jargon as the fur ball or the knife fight. All of a sudden, such ancient warrior attributes as eyesight, reflexes, and eye-hand co-ordination become paramount.

Assuming that the levels of training, experience, skill, and courage are equal among opponents, the outcome may hinge on the performance envelope of the aircraft. As antiquated as proficiency in hammerhead turns may appear in this era of gee-whiz gadgetry, the ability to execute such a manoeuvre in a more rapid and controlled manner than one's adversary may make the difference between victory or defeat, life or death.

In June 1986, a collaborative endeavour was officially begun on a new X-plane programme to explore an expansion of the fighter manoeuvrability envelope. The testbed, designated the X-31A/EFM (Enhanced Fighter Manoeuvrability), was the first in the famous American X-plane pedigree to have a foreign corporation participating as co-prime contractor.

Munich-based Messerschmitt-Boelkow-Blohm (MBB), a unit of Deutsche Aerospace (DASA), teamed with Rockwell International's North American Aircraft to produce two flying demonstrators. In 1992, a sweeping corporate reorganization at DASA's parent company, Daimler-Benz, eliminated the MBB identity and consolidated virtually all aircraft-related activities under the DASA name. German participation in the X-31 programme was made possible by the legislative "Nunn-Quayle Initiative" which encourages the U.S. and its NATO allies to increasingly

Opposite: The Rockwell/Deutsche Aerospace X-31A Enhanced Fighter Manoeuvrability (EFM) demonstrator is the first truly international X-plane programme in U.S. history. The two purpose-built experimental planes are designed to remain controllable even after they exceed their aerodynamic lift limit flying at extremely high angles of attack (AOA). An AOA of 70 degrees was reached on 18 September 1992.

X-31A
Enhanced Fighter Maneuverability
Demonstrator Aircraft

co-operate in weapons systems development.

Prior to the formalization of the German-American venture, studies by the two main participants showed that a canard/delta design incorporating a thrust vectoring system would provide the most desirous results. On 1 March, 1990, the streamlined X-31 was rolled out and on 11 October, 1990, it climbed into the sky for the first time. Just over a year later, the flight test programme was moved from Rockwell's Palmdale, California complex to NASA's Dryden Flight Research Center at nearby Edwards Air Force Base.

All along, in accordance with a carefully orchestrated plan, the aircraft has nibbled closer to its performance design limits, attempting to demonstrate controllability at extremely high angles of attack (AOA). The term angle of attack refers to the angle of an aircraft's wing relative to its actual flight path.

At this writing, the X-31 flight test programme has been postponed, awaiting an infusion of additional funds. Prior to the

61

Above: Since its maiden flight on 11 October 1990, the X-31 has been engaged in an extensive flight test programme geared towards expanding its envelope with ever-higher AOA flight. Despite the manoeuvrability of the aircraft in the post-stall regime, it has very high take-off and landing speeds of 165 to 170 knots. Flight testing has occurred at Rockwell's Palmdale, California complex and at NASA's Dryden Flight Research Center at nearby Edwards Air Force Base.

recent postponement, the X-31 was flown in mock dogfights against an F/A-18. When the X-31 employed its special manoeuvring capability, it racked up an impressive kill/loss ratio of nearly 10 to 1. There is obviously a desire to further evaluate the aircraft's tactical utility. The U.S. Navy is serving as the agent for the Advanced Research Projects Agency (ARPA), the X-31 programme manager. (Immediately upon taking office in January 1993, the new American administration retitled the Defense Advanced Research Projects Agency, eliminating the word "Defense" from the organization's name, to reflect the new emphasis on facilitating technology transfer to the civilian world.)

The configuration of the X-31 has its origins in the German concept for the European Fighter Aircraft (EFA), a consortium programme that has felt the strain of budget pressures and that is now known as Eurofighter 2000. On the one hand, the DASA and Rockwell designers

sought to create a manoeuvrability testbed, but on the other hand wanted a plane with the speed of real world fighters. This requirement for balance made it clear that the clipped double delta wing which can enable supersonic flight needed inboard and outboard elevons as well as inboard and outboard leading edge flaps.

To attain high AOA, the X-31 needed a thrust vectoring system. Based on the system installed in an F-14 spin test aircraft, three carbon/carbon composite paddles were fitted to the base of the X-31 using titanium fasteners. The rearward engine exhaust can be vectored right, left, up, or down by the paddles entering the exhaust stream as commanded by the pilot's inputs into the digital fly-by-wire (FBW) flight control system.

The aircraft would be exploring the far reaches of AOA in what is referred to as high alpha flight. Recovering from these extreme attitudes where the X-31 would fly past its aerodynamic lift limits was quite naturally a major design consideration. The all-moving canards are the answer. They provide the downward pitch control authority (as much as 50 degrees) to lower the nose when recovering from high AOA manoeuvring. In addition, a last-resort spin recovery parachute is installed in the fairing at the base of the rudder. To compensate for the reduced airflow at high AOA, the movable engine inlet lip can incline downwards 26 degrees.

A performance limiter is designed into the X-31 for safety. Certain criteria such as altitude and throttle setting must be met before the aircraft will exceed the normal maximum AOA of 30 degrees. Even then, the pilot must activate the post-stall system using a switch located mid-way down the control stick grip.

Ordinarily, when an aircraft reaches its critical AOA, it aerodynamically stalls with an attendant reduction in or loss of control. The X-31 seeks to change that with its thrust vectoring and advanced FBW flight control system. By retaining control in the post-stall regime, the X-31 can continue to turn tightly when conventional aircraft in the same regime must wait for restoration of sufficient lift. This post-stall controllability, if attainable, would provide a manoeuvring advantage during close-in air-to-air combat.

Success in achieving the research programme's objectives may lead to future fighters with improved dogfighting prowess. In essence, the X-31 is trying to prove that it is possible to turn and point more quickly than present-day fighters. On 18 September, 1992, in a flight test programme milestone, the X-31 reached an AOA of 70 degrees for the first time. A little over half a year later, on 29 April, 1993, as reported by *Aviation Week & Space Technology*, the X-31 made history again with the successful execution of the Herbst manoeuvre, a kind of hammerhead turn that entails a rapid 180 degree reversal in an extremely tight radius during post-stall flight. The manoeuvre is named in honour of Wolfgang Herbst, a deceased German pilot who inspired this research into post-stall manoeuvring. If the sought after funds are obtained to continue the flight test programme, the X-31 may be

flown with its vertical tail removed. In this case, the aircraft would rely to an even greater extent on its thrust vectoring system for control authority.

Since the two X-31s are experimental aircraft designed expressly to research enhanced fighter manoeuvrability, the lead contractors opted to proceed using off-the-shelf equipment as much as possible. For example, the canopy, windshield, and ejection seat come from the F/A-18; the fuel pumps, nose wheel tyres, and rudder pedals are those of the F-16. In total, 43 per cent of the aircraft by weight is made from off-the-shelf equipment. This heavy application of existing equipment, not least the General Electric F404 engine, serves to simplify design, lower construction costs, ease serviceability, and reduce programme risks.

Concurrently, at NASA's Langley Research Center in Virginia, a related research effort has been undertaken involving a 27 per cent scale model of the X-31, weighing 525 lb. In tests, this model was dropped from a Bell 204B helicopter and remotely piloted by NASA personnel in an electronically-linked ground station. Valuable insights into the X-31's expected flight performance and spin characteristics have been provided by the drop model test series.

Assuming no meaningful degradation of flight performance because of the add-ons to enable post-stall controllability, common sense dictates that future fighters should have the envelope-expanding capability built-in. Even if weapons technology advances to where BVR combat becomes commonplace, it is good insurance to possess a superior manoeuvring capability to handle the fur ball.

The Lockheed and Northrop teams competing for the Air Force Advanced Tactical Fighter contract recognized the value of enhanced fighter manoeuvrability. Both the YF-22 and the YF-23 prototypes incorporated thrust vectoring. Indeed, the fly-off winner, the YF-22, reached an AOA of 60 degrees. With the Air Force's next generation fighter incorporating EFM qualities, the X-31 programme may offer insight as to how such qualities can be refined and most effectively utilized.

CHAPTER 9
Yak-141: Supersonic V/STOL

Below: The main lift/cruise engine is the 34,100 lb. thrust after-burning Soyuz R 79. It is located between the twin tail booms and has a large blast deflector that deploys when the aircraft is in hover. Two lift-only 9,370 lb. thrust Rybinsk RD 41 engines have blast deflectors on both sides. They can be seen on the underside aft of the nosewheel. Also evident is the opened intake door above the lift-only engines. The Yak-141 prototype at Farnborough flew only once. Its take-off and landing were conventional, perhaps out of concern for the potential damage to the aircraft and the runway due to the extremely hot and powerful exhaust stream in hover.

Combining supersonic cruise performance with vertical/short take-off and landing (V/STOL) capability has long been a dream of the aviation design community and the military services, particularly naval air arms given the limited deck space of ships. The first to successfully meld these two extremes in an aircraft's flight envelope is the Moscow-based Yakovlev Design Bureau. (In autumn 1992, the bureau's products began to be marketed under the banner of Yak Aircraft Corporation.) Designated the Yak-141 (NATO codename Freestyle), this supersonic V/STOL is an outgrowth of the Yak-38 (NATO codename Forger).

A rather primitive answer to the British Aerospace and McDonnell Douglas Harrier, the Yak-38, operating from *Kiev* class carriers, nevertheless, gave the Soviet Navy a V/STOL fighter. The Yak-141 prototype, although far from ideal, represents a giant leap beyond its immediate predecessor. The Yak-141 is the only aircraft to have demonstrated V/STOL flight and to have cruised at supersonic speed. Reports indicate that the Yak-141 has thus far reached a top speed of Mach 1.8, proving

that Mach numbers associated with high performance air superiority fighters are within the grasp of V/STOL aircraft. The Yak-141 also set a climb record for its class — to 39,370 feet in 116 seconds.

Four Yak-141 prototypes were built; two for flight tests and two for static tests. Flight testing began in March 1989 and continued for about two years. The programme included approximately 250 flights and Yak engineers claimed success. However, the second prototype was seriously damaged while landing on the carrier *Kuznetsov* on 5 October, 1991.

Just before the aircraft plunged onto the carrier's deck, one of the new systems got an unexpected test. The Yak-141 is equipped with a Zvezda K-36 zero-zero ejection seat that is automatically activated if the aircraft exceeds predetermined flight limits in the hover mode. The automatic pilot ejection system functioned as advertised, saving the pilot's life. Cause of the accident was traced to an easily correctable design flaw in the tension of the throttle lever's detent stops. Reportedly, the damaged prototype was substantially repaired but not returned to flying status.

The Yak-141 has one rear-mounted Soyuz R 79 afterburning engine with a maximum thrust of 34,100 lb. This lift/cruise engine's nozzle can rotate 95 degrees and is partially screened from infrared detection by the twin tail booms. The afterburner may be used not only for cruise flight, but for hover as well. There are two Rybinsk RD 41 lift-only engines immediately aft of the cockpit that vector exhaust downwards for hover. These engines produce 9,370 lb of thrust each.

Air bleed ejectors are mounted on the tips of the tail booms of the remaining flying prototype. These provide yaw control during hover. The number two prototype, which crashed, incorporated some improvements, and had a single nose-mounted thruster for enhanced yaw control.

Among the drawbacks in the design of the Yak-141 is the enormous heat build-up on the underside of the aircraft during

vertical take-off and landing. In hover, the extremely powerful exhaust stream can stir up pebbles and the like, causing severe foreign object damage. Blast deflectors are located forward of the main lift/cruise engine nozzle and on both sides of the lift-only engine nozzles.

Like many military development programmes in Russia, government funding for the Yak-141 was eliminated. Yakovlev has continued the programme on its own, and has expressed a willingness to enter into a joint development with a deep-pocketed partner. There is hope that traditional purchasers of Soviet fighters, like India, may have an interest in fostering the Yak-141 and acquiring it for their forces.

Latest word from Russia was that the Yak-38 would be retired around the turn of the century and that the *Kiev* class carriers, on which Yak-38s operate, then would be converted to helicopters exclusively. The new *Kuznetsov* class of supercarriers has adopted the Sukhoi Su-27D, a navalized version of the impressive Flanker. There does not appear to be a place for the Yak-141 in the Russian Navy. There have been hints, though, that the Yak-141 could find its way into Russian Army service as a forward-based close air support fighter.

In any case, the Yak-141 would have to undergo extensive additional development

Above: In the flight test programme, the Yak-141 was reported to have achieved a speed of Mach 1.8. At Farnborough, the first prototype demonstrated supreme agility in a brief aerobatic routine. The Yak-141 may be a harbinger of even more sophisticated supersonic V/STOL aircraft that could advance beyond the prototype stage and become operational fighters, dramatically altering the framework and logistical sphere in which air defence fighters operate.

Below: Displayed for the first time in the West at the 1992 Farnborough Air Show, the number one prototype Yak-141 was clearly superior to its V/STOL predecessor, the Yak-38. With the Yak-141, supersonic flight has been merged with V/STOL capability. Practicable supersonic V/STOL could revolutionise air combat. The fastest and most capable air defence fighters would not need big air bases with long runways or supercarriers.

with system changes before entering service in a modern air force or navy. But it is a credit to the Yakovlev personnel that they were the first to produce a flying supersonic V/STOL. At the least, the generally successful flight testing of the Yak-141 signals that practicable supersonic V/STOL fighters are on the way.

CHAPTER 10
ASTOVL: Redefining Fighters

Concerned that enemy strikes against air bases may restrict or deny runway use in future wars, some military planners have their hopes set on development of an advanced short take-off and vertical landing (ASTOVL) fighter. Sometimes referred to as the STOVL strike fighter (SSF), this aircraft would be endowed with virtually all the attributes of a next generation fighter like the F-22 plus the ability to operate from extremely short surfaces.

Runway denial weapons promise to be more effective in the future. Not only may there be more powerful explosive weapons that would obliterate huge swaths of concrete, but "non-destructive" agents that would coat runways making them super slippery or sticky for long periods of time. Such devastating weapons would render conventional aircraft useless.

In early 1992, British Aerospace and McDonnell Douglas announced their co-operation on an ASTOVL fighter development programme. Interestingly, both companies have extensive experience producing the Harrier line of V/STOL fighters. Other companies exploring the ASTOVL fighter concept are Grumman (slated to be acquired by Northrop), Boeing, and Lockheed. (General Dynamics was independently involved before its announced corporate link with Lockheed.) The project is being overseen by an international group that includes the Advanced Research Projects Agency (ARPA), the U.S. Navy, NASA, and the British Royal Navy.

The design driver (and hurdle) is the propulsion system. The two main contenders at this point are derivatives of General Electric's YF120 and Pratt & Whitney's F119, the engines that faced off in the Advanced Tactical Fighter competition. Current thinking is that these powerplants would be coupled to either a shaft-driven remote lift fan or to a gas-driven lift fan. Other propulsion technologies may be explored as well. Also, Rolls-Royce and Allison may be involved. Programme goals call for an empty weight not exceeding 24,000 lb and a size not exceeding that of an F/A-18. The aircraft, as conceived, would have a single engine.

In March, ARPA awarded concept/validation contracts of approximately $30 million each to two contractor teams led by McDonnell Douglas and Lockheed, respectively. Over the ensuing three years each contractor team is expected to demonstrate its proposed propulsion system and to test large scale models in wind tunnels. If at least one of the concepts looks feasible, the programme may get the go-ahead for two flying prototypes. It should be borne in mind that the Russian Yak-141, a V/STOL fighter prototype, has already flown at supersonic speeds.

The ASTOVL fighter's primary roles would be sea-going air defence and close air support. It would also be expected to fly air interdiction, defence suppression, and reconnaissance missions. Along with an internally mounted 20mm gun, it would be expected to carry both heat-seeking and radar-guided air-to-air missiles. In order to minimize its radar cross section (RCS), missile carriage would at least be

Below: In this concept of an ASTOVL fighter's engine, a gas-driven lift system is employed. For hover and vertical landing, exhaust gases are shifted from the primary nozzle (on the right) to the lift system. The exhaust gases are then channelled by vectoring nozzles or other means to provide lift.

Below: Boeing's Military Airplanes Division has been independently pursuing its own ASTOVL design in conjunction with engine manufacturers General Electric, Pratt & Whitney, and Rolls-Royce. The Boeing concept would make extensive use of knowledge gained from the company's involvement as a partner in the F-22 programme. Various state-of-the-art components of the F-22 would be incorporated into the Boeing ASTOVL. Boeing proposes to make its ASTOVL much lighter than the F-22 with far greater use of composite materials. Note the extensive trailing edge wing flaps and the nozzle door/blast deflector open at the bottom of the mid-fuselage to accommodate the vertical lift propulsion system.

conformal. To extend range, there would probably be provision for carriage of conformal fuel tanks.

Ideally, the ASTOVL fighter would incorporate additional low observables and possess supercruise (supersonic flight without afterburner) capability. It should be able to manoeuvre as effectively as conventional air superiority fighters, perhaps more so because of its unique propulsion system. It should be remembered that the Harrier's utility in air-to-air combat was deftly illustrated during the Falklands War. Its thrust vectoring nozzles provided certain advantages during air combat manoeuvring.

Most importantly, the ASTOVL fighter will take-off with a full load of weapons and fuel in a very short distance and, with

a depleted payload, land vertically. If such an aircraft emerges from these conceptual stages, it could revolutionize the U.S. carrier fleet. Assuming attack and support planes could be adapted to the propulsion system, the supercarrier could become a relic. No longer would the big deck be necessary. Instead, equally capable aircraft could operate from smaller ships. In addition to being smaller, these ships would be faster, a performance factor contributing to enhanced survivability.

The earliest an operational ASTOVL fighter could be fielded is around the year 2010. By that time both U.S. and British Harriers will have to be replaced. The U.S. Air Force may consider the ASTOVL fighter as a candidate for its new multirole fighter, replacing the F-16.

Left: This Lockheed concept of an advanced short take-off and vertical landing (ASTOVL) strike fighter shows an aircraft influenced by the design of the company's F-22 Advanced Tactical Fighter. The wing is diamond-shaped with long-span leading edge slats, and there is provision for folding the wings. The twin vertical tail surfaces are canted outward. Canards aft of the cockpit would contribute to lift and control authority. Although the aircraft's underside is obscured, the main engine air inlet is on the bottom of the fuselage. In the scenario depicted, the fighter is flying low over a raging battle, not emitting smoke or contrails as part of its low observability. The U.S. Navy and British Royal Navy are pursuing the ASTOVL fighter concept as a possible replacement for the Harrier. The U.S. Air Force is monitoring the programme's progress with the idea that it might fulfil the requirement for the service's new multi-role fighter.

Left: This artist's depiction of the McDonnell Douglas entry in the ASTOVL competition shows a multi-role fighter with a slender fuselage profile, clearly configured to maximise low observables. Plans call for this aircraft to employ a gas-driven propulsion system utilising a derivative of the General Electric YF120 engine. For short take-offs and vertical landings, nozzles similar to those of the Harrier II will be used to vector engine exhaust. Also, a fuselage-mounted fan, powered by compressed air from the engine's exhaust, will provide vertical lift. Not surprisingly, British Aerospace and Rolls-Royce, originators of the battle-proven Harrier and its successful V/STOL propulsion system, are part of the McDonnell Douglas ASTOVL team. It should be noted that in this painting both a helicopter assault ship and a supercarrier are shown, suggesting that the McDonnell Douglas ASTOVL would be equally at home operating aboard either type of ship.

CHAPTER 11
Evolutionary Hornet: Bigger and Better

Planners for the U.S. Navy and Marine Corps, like their counterparts at the Air Force and Army, must confront the inescapable reality of aircraft useful life. Even with rigid manufacturing standards, inclusion of sturdy materials in the production process, continuous preventive maintenance, parts replacement, and service life extension programmes, there comes a time when an aircraft type reaches the end of its usefulness. This is all the more so in the case of carrier-based aircraft where the daily fatigue-inducing stresses are considerable. Also, the modern combat environment is susceptible to rapid change fostered by technological advances.

Currently, there are mainly three fixed-wing aircraft relied upon to deliver the Navy's and Marines' punch: the Grumman A-6 Intruder (medium attack), the Grumman F-14 Tomcat (interceptor/fleet air defence), and the McDonnell Douglas F/A-18 Hornet (multi-role strike fighter). The Navy, at one point, envisioned a completely new dedicated medium attack aircraft, a new air-to-air fighter/fleet defender based on the Air Force's Advanced Tactical Fighter (ATF), and an upgraded multi-role strike fighter.

Largely because of budget pressures, the outlook for naval aviation's future aircraft mix is less ambitious. Rather than maintaining the three major types, the Navy plans to whittle the number down to just two. Consideration of a Naval ATF was abandoned. Each of the remaining types is expected to be adept in both the air-to-air and air-to-surface missions. One will provide the high-end of the mix with emphasis on the surface attack role while the other will provide the low-end of the mix with roughly equal emphasis on both roles.

In one of the more intense airframe competitions in memory, Grumman and McDonnell Douglas, both with historic roots in naval aviation, opposed each other vigorously for the low-end component of the future aircraft mix. Grumman offered an improved version of its highly regarded Tomcat, modified to carry a heavy load of air-to-surface weapons (something the existing F-14 was generally not capable of doing as the aircraft was designed expressly as an air-to-air fighter). McDonnell Douglas offered a substantially upgraded version of its current multi-role Hornet strike fighter.

There was concerted lobbying by both sides, with each contractor presenting valid arguments. Ultimately, the Navy opted for the Hornet upgrade. It appears that the F/A-18's current status as a multi-role strike fighter, its design being newer than the F-14's, and its comparatively lower operational costs were deciding factors.

The fleet's Intruders are scheduled to be retired early, temporarily depriving the Navy of its deep strike capability. As a stopgap measure, the Navy's existing F-14 Tomcat air superiority fighters are being modified to carry some air-to-ground ordnance, and thus, are taking on the added nickname of Bombcat. With the modifications completed, the F-14s become multi-role fighters.

The Navy is expected to regain its deep strike capability when an Intruder replacement is fielded, but this probably will not happen until well into the next century. The Intruder's replacement will be required to possess both an air-to-air and an air-to-ground fighting capability. When this aircraft eventually enters service, the then aged Bombcat will be ripe for retirement. The Hornet upgrade, by then integrated into the fleet, will labour on as the low-end component while the new deep strike attack/fighter will serve as the high-end component.

The Hornet upgrade, designated the F/A-18E/F, promises to be a low-risk programme as it will build on the solid foundation of the current F/A-18C/D which, of course, followed the original F/A-18A/B. In keeping with the designation pattern of the earlier models, the "E" will be a single-seat aircraft and the "F" will be a two-seat aircraft.

The F/A-18 first entered fleet service in the early 1980s and soon, through outstanding operational performance, quelled concerns that had been raised about costs, deliveries, and capabilities during development. The Hornet's advertised prowess in both air-to-air and air-to-surface scenarios proved accurate. By the late 1980s, improved versions of the aircraft, the C/D configurations, were joining the inventory. These newer models incorporated such improvements as an expanded attack envelope to include the night and a high-tech reconnaissance capability. There were other enhancements in avionics and weapons systems.

A far-reaching enhancement programme currently undergoing testing for the C/D configurations is the Multi-Source Integration (MSI) software package. This programme update seeks to integrate the input from various onboard sensors such as the radar and the forward-looking infrared (FLIR) system as well as with remotely located sensors such as might be mounted on another aircraft or a ship at sea. The data from the sensors would be fused together and displayed simultaneously in a simple format.

With the combined data presented in a single, overlapping display, increasingly complex air-to-air threats could be more effectively detected, tracked, and targeted. This software will be able to relay the combined data to the F/A-18's radar-guided air-to-air missiles after launch, directing them to the target in a fashion known as launch and steer. Weapons precision will improve. Moreover, this software package will add to the pilot's situational awareness.

The MSI software will not be ready for operational use until towards the end of the decade. By then, the C/D configurations will have matured to where further enhancement with additional systems will be severely limited. Here, then, is the case

Below: The McDonnell Douglas F/A-18E/F Hornet, a larger and updated version of the earlier F/A-18A/B and F/A-18C/D Hornets, has a projected external payload capacity of 17,750 lb, approximately 30 percent more. This model of the single-seat F/A-18E is carrying heat-seeking AIM-9 Sidewinders on the wingtips, four radar-guided AIM-120 AMRAAMs (one of which is not readily visible), four 2,000 lb. Mk-84 bombs, and a centreline fuel tank.

Above: This artist's impression provides a view of the overhead planform. Because the future Hornet is scaled up from the existing design, it is difficult without a reference point to discern differences between the new and old. Note the long-span downward deflections of control surfaces along the wing's leading and trailing edges, which enhance controllability in certain flight regimes. Also note the barrels of the nose-mounted A61A1 20mm Gatling gun. The aircraft depicted here is painted in standard U.S. Navy low visibility grey. The resemblance to the existing design is strong, indeed.

for the E/F configurations. Take a proven design and, within reasonable economic parameters, scale it up to expand its capabilities.

Plans call for the F/A-18E/F to be stretched 34 inches and for the wing surface area to grow by 100 square feet or about 25 per cent. In addition to improving the aircraft's flight performance, the enlarged wing allows for two more external stores stations, bringing the total to 11. It should be noted that currently the Hornet's weapons stations can carry more types of existing ordnance than any other U.S. military aircraft. The future Hornet's added dimensions are not extreme and should not unduly complicate handling on board carriers.

The E and F models will be able to carry a maximum external load of 17,750 lb, an increase of approximately 30 per cent. Weapons with which it will be compatible include: AIM-7 Sparrow, AIM-9 Sidewinder, AIM-120 AMRAAM, Harpoon, HARM, Shrike, SLAM, Walleye, Maverick (in its TV, laser and IR versions), Advanced Interdiction Weapon System (AIWS), and an assortment of bombs and rockets. The design upgrade allows for an increase of 50 per cent in payload returnable to the carrier.

Internal fuel capacity increases by 3,600 lb or approximately 33 per cent. Also, significant quantities of additional fuel

may be carried in external tanks. The aircraft will also be capable of carrying an aerial refuelling package on its fuselage centreline pylon.

The greater fuel capacity gives the E/F configurations a vastly expanded mission radius. For example, McDonnell Douglas estimates that on an interdiction mission, the future Hornets will be able to fly 35 per cent farther than current models. Also, the extra fuel increases endurance, an important factor when flying combat air patrol (CAP). Here, the company forecasts that on a CAP 200 nautical miles from ship the E/F configurations can remain on station 80 per cent longer.

Of course, the MSI software will be available to the E and F models. The future Hornet will have an advanced cockpit with a larger, six inch square tactical situation display that projects a colour digital map overlaid with the integrated MSI data. This display promises to give the pilot/crew a comprehensive sense of the current real world environment surrounding the aircraft.

While workload should remain manageable with such innovations as a touchscreen up-front display, there are missions in which the two-seat F model would be preferrable. When, for instance, the objective is a highly-defended ground target selected for night attack, the second set of hands, eyes, and ears would come in very useful.

A major upgrade already underway is the scheduled June 1994 delivery of the first Hughes APG-73 multi-mode radar. This radar is an improved version of the APG-65 radar and boasts enhanced speed and memory of the signal and data processors. Overall, commonality in avionics and weapons systems between the forthcoming and current Hornet models exceeds 90 per cent. Like its predecessors, the E/F configurations will allow for growth in systems into the following few decades. This flexibility will enable the E/F configurations to cope with changes in the perceived threats.

The E and F models will be powered by twin F414-GE-400 afterburning turbofans.

The F414 is a derivative of the F404 which General Electric developed for the original F/A-18. The new engine can produce a whopping 22,000 lb of thrust, a leap of 35 per cent over the F404. Air inlets on the new plane will have to be enlarged to provide more airflow to the engines. It is projected that the new Hornet will have a maximum speed in excess of Mach 1.8.

Other advantages of the F414 are that it will provide a higher thrust-to-weight ratio and yet improve specific fuel consumption. The engine has been designed to better tolerate foreign object damage (FOD). There are fewer parts in certain sections because of innovations like the use of unitized blisk assemblies. In time, this engine which promises more thrust, simplified maintenance, and greater reliability may find application to other future fighters in addition to the new Hornet.

Stealth is a feature not high on the future Hornet's priority list. It is an evolutionary design that originated prior to the emergence of practical modern stealth technology. Its extensive weapons load carried externally will impede attempts to minimize the aircraft's radar cross section (RCS). New weapons should give it a fairly long beyond visual range (BVR) capability in air-to-air combat. For surface attack against a sophisticated enemy, it will have to rely on longer range stand-off weapons. Also, the high-end component of the carrier's aircraft mix could pave the way (much as the Stealth fighter did for less high-tech aircraft during 'Operation Desert Storm'), leaving clear aerial pathways for "bomb trucks" to saturate designated target areas.

The E/F configurations ought to demonstrate the same versatility as earlier model Hornets. The range of missions includes fleet air defence, air superiority, fighter escort, defence suppression, reconnaissance, forward air control, close air support, and ground/sea attack. To its credit, the McDonnell Douglas design team has retained an internally mounted cannon in the new aircraft. It is a lightweight M61A1 20mm Gatling gun with 400 rounds of ammunition. Despite the high-tech advances in weapons systems, fighter pilots still like having the last form of self-protection in the event of close-in air-to-air combat.

The E/F configurations have evolved from an existing battle-tested design. An aircraft conceived from scratch would be the preferred route, but today's economics dictate otherwise. The new Hornet has limitations, but then quite obviously it is a compromise. Such are the alternatives facing military and policy planners.

First flight of the new Hornet is scheduled for 1995. At that time it may look from a distance as if it is identical to earlier models, but it will be an improved and more capable big brother. Flying in conjunction with a genuine next generation multi-role combat aircraft like the JAST (the probable high-end component of the new mix), it should contribute to mission success. There has even been talk that the E and F models might fill the Air Force's requirement for its new multi-role fighter.

Below: An upgrade and not a true new generation multi-role strike fighter, the F/A-18E depicted in this artist's impression confirms its lineage by carrying weapons and certain systems externally and thereby increasing, not reducing, its radar cross section (RCS). This aircraft has 11 external stores stations compared to the nine of its predecessors. In addition to its heavy assortment of air-to-air and air-to-ground ordnance, the future Hornet carries a targeting FLIR (forward-looking infrared) pod affixed to its port nacelle stores station. Although out of sight, the starboard nacelle stores station has a navigation FLIR pod affixed. The new twin F414-GE-400 afterburning turbofan engines generate up to 22,000 lb thrust each. Air inlets have been enlarged to provide more airflow to the engines.

CHAPTER 12
ARES Mud Fighter:
Close Air Support Demonstrator

Opposite: Named after the Greek god of war and representing an acronym derived from the title Agile Responsive Effective Support, the ARES is another in the long and distinguished line of innovative aircraft to come from Burt Rutan's prolific Scaled Composites design boutique in Mojave, California. Developed as a fighter for the close air support (CAS) mission and for anti-helicopter warfare, the ARES with its trademark canard bears some unmistakably similar traits of earlier Rutan designs for the general aviation market. The aircraft is made mainly of lightweight composites and has a single jet engine fed by an air inlet on the port side of the fuselage. Flight tests showed that the ARES was incredibly manoeuvrable with a turn rate superior to some of the most sophisticated modern jet fighters.

From the fertile design centre of Burt Rutan's Scaled Composites, Incorporated in Mojave, California, has come another in a long line of unconventionally configured aircraft. Noted for designing a popular series of homebuilt general aviation aircraft that were made out of lightweight composite materials and that had as their trademark aft-mounted engines with pusher propellers and forward control surfaces known as canards, Rutan has gained a reputation as a trend-setting maverick.

In the early 1980s, Rutan was approached by a couple of Army aviators concerned over their perception of an increasingly sophisticated Soviet air/land threat and the helicopter's intrinsic limitations in both air-to-air combat and in providing close air support (CAS). Believing that a fixed-wing aircraft in place of or integrated with helicopters could through its superior speed overcome the disadvantages of rotary-wing aircraft, they sought the expertise of Rutan.

The first concept used a helicopter engine to drive a pusher propeller. The aircraft was a fixed-wing turboprop pusher with a canard. Called the Low-Cost Battlefield Attack Aircraft (LCBAA), the demonstrator proved to be a good all-round design.

However, there were doubts about the propeller of an aircraft assigned to the 'mud fighter' mission. A propeller would be prone to damage with the aircraft operating from unimproved airfields and it would also be subjected to possibly intolerable stress loads during air combat manoeuvring. Accordingly, the decision was made to switch to a pure jet, using the 2,900 lb thrust Pratt & Whitney Canada JT15D-5 which powers the Beechjet corporate transport and its military cousin,

the T-1A Jayhawk trainer. The aircraft became known officially as Model 151 and the name was changed to Light Attack Turbofan Single (LATS). Eventually, the current name of ARES was adopted. In Greek mythology, it is the name of the god of war. It is also the acronym for Agile Responsive Effective Support.

Rutan designs are best known for their forgiving flight characteristics, particularly their stall/spin resistance. The ARES's canard (which contains the elevators and which was swept slightly forward so it could be mounted aft of the pilot's cockpit position) stalls, predictably, when it reaches its critical angle of attack, then the aircraft pitches nose-down preventing the main wing from ever reaching its critical angle of attack and stalling. This built-in safety factor is particularly relevant for airmen flying low to the ground in a hostile environment where extreme manoeuvring may be necessary.

Like the Fairchild Republic A-10 Thunderbolt II, the ARES was designed around an anti-armour Gatling gun, only in the case of the ARES the gun is the smaller five-barrel General Electric GAU-12/U 25mm cannon. Instead of being nose-mounted, the GAU-12/U is located in a deep well on the starboard side of the forward fuselage. For the ARES, the gun's fire rate was reduced from 4,000 rounds per minute to 1,800 rounds per minute. Gun-related ammunition in the ARES totals just 220 rounds. The aircraft can also carry four Stingers and two Sidewinders for self-protection against air-to-air threats.

Static and airborne firings of the 25mm cannon were conducted. A major question was how the extremely light (6,500 lb gross weight) and radically constructed aircraft (composed of urethane foam, fibreglass, Kevlar, and low-temperature cured epoxy) would stand up to the pounding of the gun which produces an average recoil of 7,000

Right: The overhead profile shows the fuselage offset three degrees to the left of the aircraft centreline. This is to accommodate the powerful recoil of the 25mm cannon mounted in a deep well on the starboard side of the fuselage. To avoid gun gas ingestion, the engine air inlet is located on the port side. Note in the overhead profile that the engine is mounted eight degrees to the left in order to more efficiently accept the incoming air. Engine exhaust is channelled through a curved tailpipe.

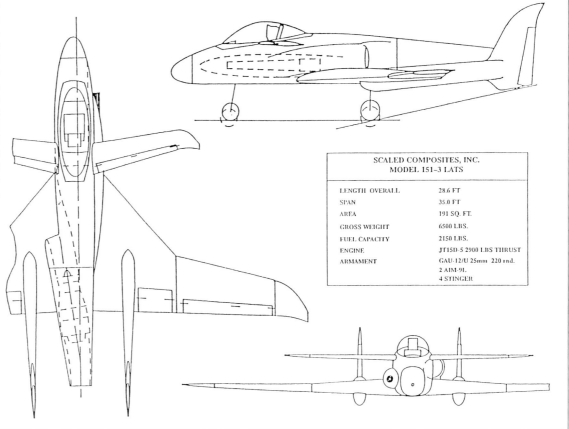

SCALED COMPOSITES, INC. MODEL 151-3 LATS	
LENGTH OVERALL	28.6 FT
SPAN	35.0 FT
AREA	191 SQ. FT.
GROSS WEIGHT	6500 LBS.
FUEL CAPACITY	2150 LBS.
ENGINE	JT15D-5 2900 LBS THRUST
ARMAMENT	GAU-12/U 25mm 220 rnd. 2 AIM-9L 4 STINGER

lb and a 100 psi muzzle blast pressure. The tests showed that the unconventional materials withstood the powerful loads generated by the gun.

As a means of reducing the impact of the gun's recoil, the gun is inserted laterally deep into the fuselage. Also, the fuselage is offset three inches to the left of the aircraft centreline.

Another major question involving the gun was whether the gases produced as a normal consequence of firing would interfere with engine operation. Gas ingestion, in fact, was an early problem for the A-10. The Rutan solution was to place the engine air inlet on the port side of the fuselage, as far removed from the gun gases as possible.

The engine, therefore, was placed in the fuselage at an eight degree angle, facing towards the inlet on the side of the aircraft. A curved tailpipe is installed to direct the exhaust straight out the tail. This highly unusual arrangement succeeded in keeping gun gases away from the engine air inlet, even when firing at high angles of attack.

The ARES is a conceptually advanced aircraft, but certain of its components reveal a low budget programme and a common Rutan practice of keeping equipment and systems as simple as possible. For example, the ARES cockpit has nothing more advanced than an off-the-shelf head-up display (HUD) and an older zero/zero ejection seat. Instrumentation is strictly standard general aviation dials and gauges. There is no fancy fly-by-wire (FBW) flight control system; just sturdy pushrods and mechanical linkages.

Among the ARES's performance achievements in the flight test programme which started on 19 February, 1990, is its demonstrated range of over 1,200 nautical miles. The long range can translate into extended endurance, an important consideration for CAS aircraft.

The efficient fuel burn of the engine is, of course, a contributing factor to this impressive range/endurance performance. The considerable fuel capacity contributes as well. A total of approximately 333 gallons can be held inside the wing strakes and the wing centre section. This means that the ARES can carry up to 2,200 lb of fuel, which represents about a third of the aircraft's gross weight.

The aircraft, not surprisingly, has proven able to take-off and land (with minimal payload) in only about 1,200 feet of runway. This ability is critical for any CAS aircraft since it is likely that in a real world setting it would have to operate from less than ideal remote airfields.

The most eye-catching result to emerge from the ARES's flight test programme was its demonstrated turn performance. It actually out turns some of the most sophisticated jet fighters flying today. It has the ability to turn 36 degrees per second at seven Gs. This incredible manoeuvrability is a major plus for the fighter pilot.

Scaled Composites suggests that the ARES is an appropriate candidate for CAS missions involving light armour, anti-helicopter operations, border patrol, and a number of roles required in low-intensity conflict. A proposed two-seat variant, designated the Model 151-4 LATS, is mentioned as both a forward air control plane and a tactics/proficiency trainer.

Given the likely nature of tomorrow's battlefield, it will probably be necessary for the CAS aircraft to possess great speed so that it can dash in and out of the exceptionally "down and dirty" airspace. Hostile forces must not have the opportunity to point and shoot. In the moments leading up to and during ordnance delivery the CAS aircraft may have to slow down, but this sequence would represent a minute part of the mission.

Another probable requirement is that the CAS aircraft will have to be armoured so as to prevent a "lucky" round from relatively small calibre arms causing serious harm. Ballistics tolerance will have to be built into any CAS aircraft whether helicopter, fixed-wing aircraft, or hybrid.

Also, the ideal future CAS aircraft will have a high degree of weapons systems capability. With sophisticated air-to-ground missiles it should be possible for the CAS aircraft, in certain instances, to fire at permanent or temporarily immobile enemy targets from a respectable distance, reducing its exposure to hostile elements. Since hardened bunkers are among the prospective targets, air-to-ground munitions must pack a real wallop to be effective.

In the aforemetioned areas, the ARES as currently configured is somewhat questionable. The ARES lacks the high speed for the dash in and out of the fire zone. It is unclear if the composites so successful in the homebuilt general aviation market would offer adequate airframe protection against an anti-aircraft barrage. The ARES's adaptability to a larger calibre gun and heavier, more sophisticated air-to-ground weapons is doubtful.

Right: The ARES's five-barrel General Electric GAU-12/U Gatling gun was fired in static tests as well as in airborne trials to determine if the aircraft's lightweight composite structure could withstand the powerful vibrations. The materials held up under these demanding conditions. There was some yawing and pitching induced by the gun's recoil which could be corrected by installation of a blast diffuser/diverter.

In any event, the ARES is a valuable addition to the progression towards the ideal CAS aircraft. Many of the ideas it incorporates such as use of canard surfaces, an asymmetric fuselage, and gun gas ingestion avoidance are worthwhile and deserving of further study. It may very well be that some of the innovations that Burt Rutan and his talented staff pioneered in the ARES will be incorporated in future CAS aircraft. The aerospace community owes much to Rutan's creativity. When the aeronautical genius of Mojave offers a design, industry and government should pay attention. (In 1993, Burt Rutan announced his intention to move his company to Montrose, Colorado, which offered attractive business incentives.)

CHAPTER 13
EX Concept: The Diamond Wing

For many years the U.S. Navy has recognized the burden imposed by operating many different aircraft types for the myriad missions required of a carrier-based air armada. With each aircraft type comes a dedicated parts supply network, distinctive maintenance support system, and plane-specific training programme. Clearly, it would be to the service's advantage to minimize the number of different aircraft types by incorporating as many missions as feasible into a few versatile airframes.

Indeed, the Navy pursued just such a course. The aircraft envisioned was called the Advanced Tactical Support Aircraft (ATSA). This lone aircraft type would at the least replace the Grumman E-2C Hawkeye, the Grumman EA-6B Prowler, and the Lockheed S-3 Viking. Yet, by 1991 budget ills led to the demise of this admirable effort.

The Navy's inventory of planes is not immune from the effects of ageing and with time all military aircraft, no matter how well engineered and built, reach the point when they must be replaced. Boeing's Military Airplane unit has quietly pursued a replacement for the E-2C. For now called, generically, the EX (Electronics Experimental), the Boeing platform may later serve as a replacement for other electronic warfare aircraft as well.

Ironically, Boeing's work on this project evolved in 1988 from a U.S. Air Force desire for a surveillance aircraft that could bolster the airborne warning perimeter surrounding the U.S. As the Soviet threat diminished, Air Force interest in the new high-tech platform waned. The company, not wanting to abandon what it perceived as a promising new concept, continued to pump approximately $2 million of its own money each year into its EX project.

The Boeing EX, as currently conceived, makes use of a fuselage that is remarkably similar in general outline to that of the S-3. The four-person wrapped-in-windows cockpit arrangement of two forward (presumably, pilot and navigator) and two

behind (presumably, electronics systems operators), with ejection seats for all, is reminiscent of the seating arrangement in the EA-6B. It is the concept's wing shape and use that represent a radical departure.

Called a joined wing, it is in effect a high-tech biplane design. While previous NASA studies of the joined wing revealed little aerodynamic advantage over conventional lifting surfaces, Boeing engineers perceived

Below: The Boeing EX concept sports a joined wing that forms a diamond shape. The aircraft makes use of smart structures in that the radar antenna is incorporated into the wing. Indeed, the wing also holds the radar's transmit/receive modules, power conditioning, and cooling systems. Because of the absence of obstructions, the radar does not have the same clutter interference as traditional AEW aircraft with radomes and can detect small targets at greater distances. Since this plane is perceived as being carrier-based, its wing will be capable of folding for stowage on and below deck.

a usefulness of the joined wing in the aerial electronic surveillance mission. By incorporating the advanced radar into the wing, the need for a heavy, drag-inducing overhead radome would be eliminated.

In the opinion of Boeing's design staff, technology has advanced to the point where "smart structures" may permit vastly improved operating efficiencies. The phased array radar antennas are a part of the wing. Instead of detracting from the aircraft's performance, the antennas have become a blended part of the aircraft.

Boeing has scrupulously analysed NASA's joined wing research data, and has determined that for the mission in question the aircraft will perform best with a joined wing that forms a diamond shape. This is a refinement of the NASA configurations that suggested a less symmetric shape forged by the back-swept and forward-swept wing sections. Also, the wings of the Boeing EX concept are swept a dramatic 40 degrees. While this feature may enhance cruise speeds, the stated reason for doing this was to accommodate the radar's scan.

Current AEW aircraft with mounted radomes typically incur clutter produced as a result of the interference of their wings and engines. This also impairs their ability to detect small objects.

The proposed EX overcomes these hindrances because its radar conforms to the wings. Unobstructed, full spherical coverage is afforded the antennas-in-the-wings surveillance system. Moreover, because of advances in conformal, active phased array radar technology, it now appears that not only can working radars be made to fit wings, but to extend detection ranges up to two and a half times that of the current radome system of the E–2C. Tests indicated that the new radar in the proposed EX could illuminate targets with a one square metre cross section at up to 600 nautical miles. Even small objects like cruise missiles skimming a few feet over the water could be picked up by the aircraft's sensors up to 150 nautical miles away. With the stalking anti-ship threat taking on increasing lethality, it is vital that detection ranges of AEW aircraft be extended.

The peculiar mixture of a forward wing with dihedral and an aft wing with anhedral, joined at their respective tips no less, leaves a kind of gap between them as viewed from the front of the aircraft. It is in this opening that the Boeing designers have placed the two pod-mounted engines. On pylons extending from the top of the fuselage, aft of the cockpit, the engines' air inlets are positioned to receive an unobstructed flow from over the forward wing while engine exhausts would easily pass under the aft wing.

The planned engine is the TF-34-GE-400A, which hardly by coincidence powers the S-3. This engine may be upgraded by General Electric to provide 40 per cent more thrust. Of significant value, the proposed EX would be able to operate in a wide speed range — as slow as a Mach 0.38 cruise and as fast as a Mach 0.76 sprint.

Endurance is critical for the aircraft forming the defensive outer shield of the carrier battle group. Any AEW aircraft must have a great loiter time capability. Also important is the maximum speed available for quick deployment or expedited recovery. The proposed EX, if the calculations hold true in the real world, would leave the E-2C behind in its wake. In normal configuration, when fully loaded at 56,300 lb, it is estimated to have a maximum range of 2,590 nautical miles. This could be extended to an unrefuelled range of 2,970 nautical miles with 400 gallon external fuel tanks.

As awkward as this diamond-winged concept appears, it should be taken seriously. Its creator is the same company that pioneered modern airborne early warning with its E-3 Sentry, known as AWACS (airborne warning and control system). The move by Boeing to propose a platform incorporating smart structures in place of the traditional radome is innovative and bold. It will be interesting to see if the other two leading contenders in the naval AEW sweepstakes, Grumman and Lockheed, will be content to offer upgrades of existing designs or break from the past. In the end, the Navy may end up with its long-sought multi-purpose airframe after all.

CHAPTER 14
MMSA: A Plane for All Missions

In an attempt to cut down on the number of different military aircraft types, the futurists at the Lockheed Advanced Development Company, better known as the Skunk Works, have created a multi-mission support aircraft (MMSA) concept that uses a fan-in-wing propulsion system. This jet-lift scheme, tested on the Ryan XV-5A in the 1960s and generally regarded then as infeasible, would provide a vertical take-off and landing (VTOL) capability.

Interestingly, the Lockheed concept uses a flying-wing planform not unlike that of the Northrop B-2 Stealth bomber. One might logically conclude that when the Lockheed MMSA is not in hover, it would project a minimal radar cross section (RCS). The low observables nature of this aircraft would be a major plus over conventional support aircraft types.

It is not clear if Lockheed envisions its MMSA employing smart structures. It seems that the incorporation of a radar antenna along portions of the large area wing, in similar fashion to the Boeing EX smart wing design, would be possible. With such a design, there would be no need for a mounted radome. Of course, an activated radar system would make the aircraft vulnerable to enemy detection. Perhaps a flight profile could be adopted that calls for activation of the onboard radar in irregular intervals, allowing the MMSA to revert to a stealthy mode intermittently.

In addition to its obvious applicability to electronic warfare (EW), the basic airframe of the Lockheed MMSA concept could serve in a multitude of roles such as search and rescue, special operations, and light transport. A single support aircraft type would drastically reduce the complexity and cost of the current situation involving myriad support aircraft types, each requiring its own parts supply, maintenance programme, and flight training programme.

A fairly voluminous bay in the aircraft's mid-section could be used to carry troops and/or cargo. Moreover, because this MMSA concept is a VTOL, it could replace the military's medium lift helicopters. Lockheed also suggests that its MMSA concept could be converted to a regional airliner. As such it would offer some of the advantages associated with a tilt-rotor, but would probably be capable of faster cruise speeds.

Left: The Lockheed vision of a multi-mission support aircraft (MMSA) is a flying-wing with a fan-in-wing propulsion system. If the technological hurdles associated with previously abandoned fan-in-wing propulsion systems can be surmounted, this concept would hold promise and offer a solution to the military's logistical problems in operating myriad support aircraft types. The planform, reminiscent of the Northrop B-2 Stealth bomber, probably offers similar inherently stealthy characteristics. It is perhaps not a coincidence then that the heat from the exhaust streams in this artist's impression distort the aircraft's shadow on the ground to create a silhouette that roughly matches the outline of Lockheed's F-117A Stealth fighter.

CHAPTER 15
Aurora: Classified Reconnaissance Speedster

Below: The X-30 was the proposed flying technology demonstrator for the single-stage-to-orbit National Aero-Space Plane (NASP). One of the aircraft perceived to be the Aurora, the rumoured high altitude, high speed reconnaissance aircraft, may incorporate certain of the X-30's design features such as a sharply-swept delta-style planform, engines blended into the fuselage underside, and twin vertical fins. This Aurora type may have already succeeded in achieving some of the technological breakthroughs necessary for the success of the NASP programme.

From the late 1980s into the early 1990s, there has been an increasing swirl of rumours that a mysterious high altitude, hypersonic reconnaissance aircraft, called Aurora, is performing operational missions. The first hint that such a spy plane existed came through the inadvertent release of a Pentagon budget document in 1985 that referred to a project titled Aurora, listed as being funded at a whopping $2.1 billion. This reference to Aurora followed a line item on the SR-71 Blackbird, then the world's leading spy plane and the fastest known air-breathing manned aircraft.

Speculation immediately focused on Lockheed as the Aurora's prime contractor. Not only had Lockheed's legendary Skunk Works produced the amazing Blackbird, but Aurora was the long accepted nickname given to the Canadian Forces version of the Lockheed-built Orion antisubmarine warfare (ASW) aircraft. By using an existing nickname, the company could obscure the new top secret programme.

In the ensuing years there has been a growing number of media reports that Aurora is flying. Most stories are of chance sightings from the ground and in the air. At least one relevation came in the form of a leak from military officials. In 1988, *The New York Times* quoted an unidentified government source as saying that a new aircraft was under development that would outclass the SR-71 which itself can achieve altitudes in excess of 85,000 feet and speeds of over Mach 3.

There have also been seismological recordings in Southern California pointing to the probable flight path of a hypersonic air vehicle. Moreover, some amateur radio operators monitoring military frequencies have intercepted transmissions in which the chatter involved altitudes and speeds suggestive of an exotic aircraft like the Aurora.

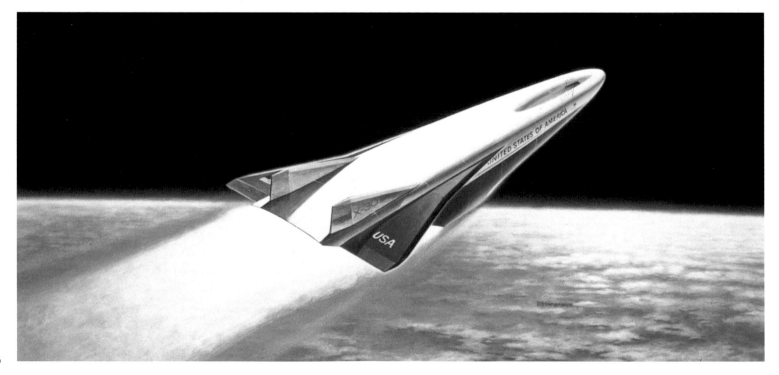

In some sighting debriefs, the presumed Aurora is described as having a shape generally in consonance with the commonly depicted planform of the X-30, the single-stage-to-orbit research vehicle that until mid-1993 was in development as a testbed for the National Aero-Space Plane (NASP) programme. It should be noted that Rockwell is a prime contractor on the NASP programme, and that, by curious circumstance, it was teamed with Lockheed's Skunk Works in the U.S. Navy's ill-fated A/F-X competition.

As of mid-1993, the U.S. government's plans changed such that the X-30 was cancelled. In its place, three different types of delta-shaped unmanned testbeds would be launched atop Minuteman and Titan boosters from Vandenburg Air Force Base in a programme known as the Hypersonic Flight Test Experiment or Hyflte. Some observers have speculated that the reason the X-30 was cancelled was not budgetary, as officially proclaimed, but because of the recognition that Aurora has already achieved much of the X-30's programme objectives.

Depending on the particular report and interpretation, the sighted aircraft is sleek with far more length than wing span. From a pointed nose the shape gradually expands rearward with a sharply-swept delta or clipped-wing design. Rectangular engine air inlets and exhaust nozzles are contained in a blended fuselage underside. Twin vertical tail surfaces are located aft and outboard. Other descriptions give the aircraft retractable canards, unfolding to provide necessary controllability in slow flight such as when landing.

Studies have shown that a delta wing with a dramatic sweep is best for flight in the hypersonic regime. The underside location of the engine is consistent with design theory of a hypersonic aircraft. As it travels through high Mach numbers extreme pressures in the form of shock waves are created. Rather than fighting this phenomenon, Aurora would take advantage of it and in effect ride the shock waves. In hypersonic flight, inlet airflow would be most efficient with this configuration.

During certain phases of flight when the aircraft's angle of attack is relatively high, the long delta shape would tend to block out airflow above, severely restricting flow across the centre of the aircraft's upper tail section. As a result, the outboard vertical fin arrangement is used.

Speeds are so great that aircraft skin temperatures become extreme. A structural material like titanium ceramic fibre composite, which was planned for the X-30, may be used. Formed in a metal matrix by hot isostatic pressure, this material offers the essentials of light weight, strength, and heat tolerance. Cooling may be accomplished through circulation of cryogenic fuel, probably either liquid hydrogen or liquid methane, acting as a heat sink.

Aurora's propulsion system is the subject of intense curiosity. It is known that on at least a few occasions aircraft have been observed since 1989 emitting concurrently the sound of periodic pulses against a constant loud background roar and the sight of a string of evenly-spaced puffs in contrails, commonly referred to as doughnuts-on-a-rope. These features suggest the use of pulsed detonation wave engines (PDWEs), cutting edge powerplants.

In a PDWE, ongoing detonations in dedicated small chambers cause supersonic shock waves to form and to rush across the engine's larger combustion chamber, compressing the fuel-air mixture and thereby producing an even greater shock wave that is then channelled rearward as exhaust. Such an engine has virtually no moving parts, and therefore, enjoys remarkably uncomplicated mechanics compared to conventional propulsion systems.

Some experimental research data have confirmed that PDWEs offer high thrust potential, fuel efficiency, relative light weight, and simplicity. Accordingly, it is believed that this engine type is a logical candidate for propelling air vehicles into the high Mach regime.

Interestingly, a PDWE should be able to burn fuel using either free-stream air or an onboard oxidizer. In theory, a PDWE can operate at any speed and at any altitude.

Under such circumstances, the need for a mother ship would be questionable. Because evidence suggests that the Aurora at times is launched from a mother ship, it appears that the Aurora is powered by a different, perhaps less radical, type of propulsion system such as a combined cycle engine. Nevertheless, it could be that the PDWEs have been retrofitted on some of the Aurora types for flight trials.

The noticeable pulsing noise and observed doughnuts-on-a-rope phenomenon may stem from the engine's variable pressure combustion process where supersonic shock waves roll in opposite directions across the main combustion chamber. In a PDWE, the thrust generated seems to be a function of the frequency of detonation. The greater the frequency of detonation, the more rapid is the occurrence of alternating shock waves.

As the name implies, the combined cycle engine brings together different engine types in the same powerplant. For flight at the lower end of Aurora's performance envelope, the combined cycle engine would make use of either turbojets or a liquid-fuelled rocket engine (for short

bursts with a minimum amount of onboard liquid oxygen as the oxidizer).

Once the aircraft speeds up to the appropriate point between Mach 2 and Mach 3, the traditional engine(s) would shut down and two or more ramjets would kick in at what for them would be minimum operational airspeed. At that point, the Aurora could begin to accelerate to its cruise speed in the neighbourhood of Mach 6. The propulsion system would work equally as efficiently for return to the home base, with the ramjets shutting down when the aircraft decelerates to below Mach 3 and at that point the traditional engine(s) starting up for a powered flight to a conventional runway landing.

Some of the loud noises attributed to the Aurora may be explained by the airflow through the ramjets' ducts. When moving at relatively low speeds, the airflow through the ducts is unable to remain continuous, causing periodic build-ups and releases of pressure that in turn result in explosive-sounding noises. These are noises distinct to ramjets travelling below their cruise speeds and are unrelated to the PDWE noises.

Upon reaching the high end of its performance envelope, the Aurora's telltale engine sounds and/or sights would not be discernible. Obviously, the aircraft is intended to remain inconspicuous over world hot spots. *Aviation Week & Space Technology* has theorized that Aurora's mission profile includes the launching of small unmanned satellites into earth orbit for reconnaissance and possibly other purposes.

Interestingly, Lockheed itself has used SR-71 variants to launch small D-21 drones. More recently, Lockheed has suggested using the remaining Blackbirds (three are operated by NASA for research) as launch platforms for small manned or unmanned vehicles. A proposed manned version called the Hypersonic Air Launch Option (HALO) would be a Mach 10-12 testbed powered in part by a scramjet (supersonic combustion ramjet) engine.

Sandia National Laboratories is reportedly developing an unmanned

Below: As shown in this chart, turbojet usefulness ends at about Mach 4. Ramjet effectiveness is estimated to extend to around Mach 6, while the scramjet (supersonic combustion ramjet) has a range of operability into far higher Mach numbers. For the highest speeds, hydrogen would be the preferred fuel. Hydrogen's advantages include its utility as a heat sink, the highest thermal stability, and outstanding burn characteristics. But methane would be the preferred fuel for an air-breather because of its easier handling qualities (in liquid form methane requires cooling to −43 degrees Fahrenheit versus −421 degrees Fahrenheit for Hydrogen) and its greater density compared to hydrogen, which allows for more onboard fuel storage in less space.

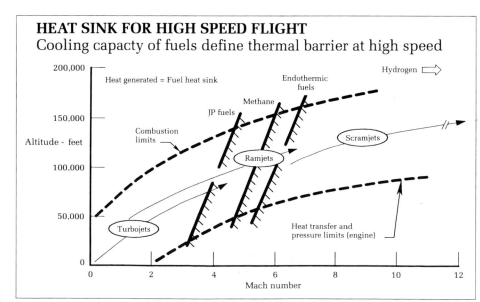

HEAT SINK FOR HIGH SPEED FLIGHT
Cooling capacty of fuels define thermal barrier at high speed

vehicle for air launch known as SAPHYRE, which would explore flight to Mach 25 — the goal set for the NASP. Proponents believe that HALO and SAPHYRE would be more useful research tools than the X-30 in perfecting the NASP.

If Aurora's designers succeeded in integrating the avionics to a new standard, it is possible that Aurora is crewed by a single pilot. Yet, because of the complexities of onboard systems, the flight envelope, and mission requirements, it seems more likely that the pilot is accompanied in tandem by a systems officer. Sensor data are probably transmitted real time or near real time directly to command and control centres/users as the aircraft's altitude would obviate the need to employ a communications satellite relay.

A possible explanation for the widely divergent descriptions is that there may be three entirely different aircraft types, which in the rush to identification, are all lumped together under the title Aurora. The first of the three exotic aircraft most probably is the Aurora. The second may be an aerial launch platform for the Aurora while the third is likely a newer version of the Aurora with even more impressive performance characteristics.

From this vantage point, the first of the Aurora types is a relatively small aircraft, perhaps the size of an F-15, with a flattened football shape. Probable first flight occurred around 1981-1983. Top speed would be about Mach 5-6. Highest altitude attainable would approach 150,000 feet. At the peak of its performance envelope, Aurora would perhaps not only transmit intelligence data, but launch small satellites and possibly even fire very high velocity weapons at high priority targets. Because the aircraft's size limits onboard fuel, Aurora would have relatively meagre endurance, a drawback for a recon-naissance aircraft.

Addressing this problem, designers may have devised a huge carrier vehicle for Aurora. Riding piggyback, Aurora would launch from the fast, high flying, and inflight refuelable carrier vehicle as it approached the relevant airspace. The launch platform is probably the large

Below: Of the three Aurora-type aircraft that are rumoured to exist, the design configuration with a flattened football shape, as depicted in this artist's rendering, is probably the first of the Aurora types. Conceivably flight tested as early as 1981, this plane would fly missions at altitudes of nearly 150,000 feet and at speeds in the range of Mach 5–6. Aurora may be launched from a large carrier aircraft, and in turn may launch small satellites into orbit. Aurora would serve primarily as a real-time and near real-time reconnaissance platform, and possibly possess a precision strike capability. However, this version's greatest contribution may have been its use as a demonstrator for a larger and more capable second-generation Aurora type.

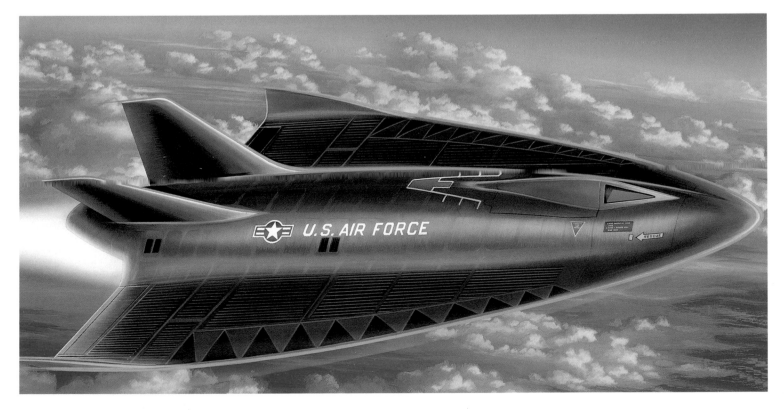

U.S. AIR FORCE

clipped delta with raised wingtips and retractable canards that has been sighted and confused with the Aurora. It probably has performance similar to the SR-71.

When the carrier nears the top of its performance envelope, the Aurora would separate. From that juncture, Aurora would have sufficient endurance to survey designated sites. The Aurora's landings, conceivably deadstick like the Space Shuttle though probably not, would be at a handful of isolated military facilities. The big carrier vehicle, possibly 200 feet long, would land conventionally at the same base. For security, virtually all operations would be conducted at night.

The final aircraft of the three appears to be of a whole new generation. This is the plane sighted from the late 1980s and described as having a dramatically swept "V" shape. It has been suggested that this extremely advanced aircraft, measuring as much as 100 feet long, might have the performance capabilities of the HALO. Even more bold is the suggestion that like the proposed SAPHYRE or X-30, it might even have a single-stage-to-orbit capability. A small onboard rocket engine could boost this Aurora type into low Earth orbit.

This newer and larger, second generation Aurora may also be launched from the mother ship. An airborne launch would not only preserve the vehicle's fuel, but would allow powered flight to get underway with the vehicle's ramjets. In theory, such an aircraft could achieve the necessary ramjet starting speed by riding piggyback on the mother ship as it accelerated to over Mach 2. While no doubt taking advantage at times of mother ship launches, the latest Aurora type is in all probability still able to operate independently using some combination of powerplants.

From its extraordinarily high perch, either in or near orbit, this aircraft/space plane would perform reconnaissance and launch small satellites into orbit. It might also possess an offensive strike capability against both airborne and ground targets. Probably only a precious few, no more than a couple dozen, of each of the three types exist.

When the Department of Defense announced the shut down of its SR-71 fleet, there were surprisingly few repercussions, and protests were unusually meek. The official line was that this highly specialized fleet was too expensive to continue to operate in a period of declining defence budgets, and an expanding network of spy satellites would fill the void.

These explanations are suspect, however. As a percentage of ongoing strategic costs, the Blackbirds' operational costs were a drop in the bucket. Also, conventionally launched satellites have long lead times and are more or less fixed in orbit. Their reconnaissance function is limited to varying degrees by the path of their orbit and the planet's weather.

An aircraft, untouchable by the enemy because of altitude and speed, that has the flexibility to overfly anywhere needed on short notice would make a valuable reconnaissance platform. It is worth noting that around the time that the SR-71s ceased flying military missions in 1990, activity attributed to Aurora picked up.

Further, SR-71s operated from Beale Air Force Base in California, a key facility for intelligence gathering that is known to still have operational U-2s, the venerable Lockheed spy planes that preceded the Blackbirds. As if fitting pieces of a puzzle, some of the Aurora-like sightings and noise observations have occurred in the vicinity of the base. Other observations have occurred near the Air Force Flight Test Center at Edwards Air Force Base, also in California, and around Tonopah and Groom Lake, Nevada, remote sites used in the past for top secret aircraft operations or testing.

It should be mentioned that yet other unconventional and exotic aircraft besides the Aurora types have been observed. These other planes are said to be startlingly gigantic, measuring up to four times the size of the largest of the three Aurora-type aircraft, and possessing rounded, triangular shapes coming close to mimicking the flying saucers of science fiction. These aircraft have reportedly been seen flying at exceptionally slow speeds and making incredibly tight turns. They also have the pulsing engines associated with Aurora. Extremely bright lights, which may be the engine exhaust plumes or glowing aircraft surfaces from the heat of hypersonic flight, are a characteristic of these aircraft. Perhaps these sightings were of the largest of the Aurora types, and due to a lack of perspective in an open night sky, dimensions and perspective became diffcult to decipher.

Despite the flurry of media reports and the rampant speculation, the Air Force continues to flatly deny the existence of Aurora or other exotic aircraft as described. In fact, it may be that the Air Force does not control these assets. Jurisdiction over the Aurora could rest with an interagency organization with major CIA participation. If Aurora is flying, as seems likely, the Air Force would retain greater credibility by

merely refusing comment upon receipt of inquiries.

There is a legitimate role for secrecy in furtherance of national security. Surely, Aurora's advanced technologies, achieved through years of quiet, painstaking research, are ahead of the technologies developed by potential adversaries, and no reasonable person would advocate wholesale disclosure resulting in a give-away. It should also be remembered that the Lockheed Skunk Works has a reputation for thriving in the ultra-classified world, left unfettered by probing government bureaucrats.

Yet, secrecy ought to be preserved only so long as it does not diminish government credibility. Benefits could accrue to many if the existence of the Aurora types was finally acknowledged and certain data declassified and properly shared. Civil programmes, especially those concerned with high altitude, high speed flight (e.g., the development of new supersonic airliners and the NASP), would gain from selective release of technological information. Applying the breakthroughs of the Aurora types to these programmes would accelerate their progress.

History may be repeating itself. A couple of years prior to the government's disclosure of the existence of the Stealth fighter, the well known plastic model company, the Testor Corporation, began marketing a kit of its conceptualization of the Stealth fighter, designed by its employee John Andrews, that turned out to be fairly accurate to the actual article. Just in time for the 1993 holiday shopping season, Testors has done it again — releasing two separate kits, also designed by John Andrews, under the title Aurora.

Testors contends that two advanced aircraft comprise the "Aurora system", which, according to the company, may instead be known as "Senior Smart" or "Senior Citizen". The first of these aircraft is what the company calls the SR-75 Penetrator; it is a huge mother ship, manned by a crew of three, that can

achieve Mach 3.5 and serve as a reconnaissance platform itself. When not carrying its Aurora sister ship, it may carry Pegasus-style booster rockets that launch small satellites into low Earth orbit. The second Testors aircraft is called the XR-7 Thunder Dart and can supposedly exceed speeds of Mach 7. The XR-7 is said to have the ability to operate completely independent of the larger launch vehicle.

The Thunder Dart, which sports a 75 degree swept delta configuration, is said to be powered by two conventional turbojets and, for high-Mach flight, two PDWEs. The model's PDWEs are pod-mounted atop the aft fuselage. This engine placement is questionable as the airflow at higher angles of attack during high speed flight would tend to be blanked out there. A more plausible scenario is that a couple of PDWEs were fitted atop an Aurora type for research purposes, and a Testors informant saw or heard about the aircraft with this arrangement. Testors suggests that the PDWEs are ignited by use of a throttle-controlled, laser-based heat source.

To its credit, Testors has thought through the escape mechanism for the XR-7's lone pilot, suggesting that the aircraft's delta-shaped nose section, which contains the cockpit, can detach and glide to a safe altitude where the pilot may then eject in a conventional fashion. Also, Testors is of the opinion, shared by many, that the Aurora types are operated under the aegis of a secretive government agency. The decals of the Thunder Dart model show it in the livery of the National Reconnaissance Office, a recently declassified U.S. government agency managing aerial spying.

Perhaps it will not be long before the world gets its first sanctioned glimpse of the Aurora types. Then, observers will be able to compare the configurations envisaged by the likes of the Testors Corporation to the real aircraft. Chances are that the speculative versions will not be too far off the mark.

CHAPTER 16
TR-3A: The Flying Triangle

Spurred on by the possibilities of stealth, in the mid-1970s the Advanced Research Projects Agency (ARPA) funded the 'Have Blue' programme aimed at producing a practical attack aircraft with an extremely low radar cross section (RCS). Both Lockheed and Northrop competed. The Lockheed design was adjudged the more capable, and two 'Have Blue' demonstrators were built. The success of these prototypes led to production of the Lockheed F-117A Stealth fighters.

Undeterred, Northrop continued its studies of stealth designs. Under the U.S. Air Force Tactical High Altitude Penetrator (THAP) programme, Northrop was known to have developed a wind tunnel test article. This model had a triangular, manta-ray shape, a variation on the flying wing planform of Northrop's B-2 Stealth bomber. However, the model's trailing edge was mildly curved, not serrated, and the points at which the leading edges merge with the

trailing edge were rounded rather than abrupt. Current visualizations of the TR-3A derive from this 1976 model.

It has been suggested that another difference between the TR-3A and its B-2 big brother is that the former has two vertical rudder-like control surfaces. Given the TR-3A's mildly curved trailing edge and the point in time when the aircraft was developed, it is indeed plausible that it would have these control surfaces for yaw authority. Roll and pitch authority come from trailing edge elevons.

As a means of minimizing the RCS of the vertical control surfaces, they are probably canted at a considerable angle. Reports suggest that they are inwardly canted. Given the TR-3A's sizable wing area and the consequent ability to place the vertical control surfaces distant from the engines' exhaust stream, this may be true. At the same time, it should be remembered that Lockheed opted to outwardly cant the

Left: In the mid-1970s, the Advanced Research Projects Agency (ARPA) proceeded with a competition between Northrop and Lockheed for a stealth aircraft. Based on results from scale model testing, the Lockheed concept was selected and two flying prototypes were ordered. Under the codename 'Have Blue', Lockheed's Skunk Works went from contract to first flight in about a year. In late 1977 or early 1978, the first 'Have Blue' demonstrator made its maiden flight. The first 'Have Blue' demonstrator confirmed the airworthiness of the design and the second verified the low observables. Because of the success of this programme, full-scale development was soon begun under the codename 'Senior Trend'.

Above: The F-117A Stealth fighter, the U.S. Air Force's attack aircraft that performed so effectively during the 1991 Persian Gulf War, evolved from the 'Have Blue' demonstrator. The F-117A is approximately twice as large as the demonstrator (which was not designed to carry weapons) and its vertical tail surfaces cant outwards instead of inwards so as not to trap the heat of engine exhaust. Some of the theory behind the Stealth fighter's faceted structure design derives from a technical paper published in 1962 by the Soviet scientist Pyotr Ufimtsev. The breakthroughs reported in that paper gave Lockheed's researchers the handle they needed to develop a practical stealth aircraft. Deliveries of the F-117A to the Air Force began in September 1982. By October of the following year, Stealth fighters based at Tonopah, Nevada were operational.

vertical control surfaces of its F-117A Stealth fighter based on the heat build-up experienced by the 'Have Blue' demonstrators that had inwardly canted vertical control surfaces.

Like the Stealth bomber, the TR-3A's engine bays are blended right into the airframe/wing. Chances are that today's operational TR-3As use non-afterburning turbofans in the same family as the General Electric F118-GE-100s that are installed in the B-2. However, since the TR-3A is smaller and reportedly has a wing span only a little over a third that of the B-2, it has two engines, not four. Exhaust flow mixers would suppress a large part of the IR signature.

The aircraft undoubtedly has a fly-by-wire (FBW) flight control system. The structure probably makes extensive use of carbon fibre materials and where

appropriate radar absorbing materials (RAM). A forward cockpit with a blended canopy is said to accommodate a lone pilot. However, there may be a second crew station in tandem given the mission's complexity.

The designation TR denotes "tactical reconnaissance", but it is not clear why this aircraft would be restricted to surveillance duties alone. While considerable internal volume is dedicated to sophisticated imaging sensors with real-time or near real-time data link equipment, carriage of a few precision-guided munitions would seem feasible.

There has been speculation that the TR-3A was deployed in 'Operation Desert Storm' as a dedicated recce platform for the Stealth fighters. In this capacity, the TR-3As would have been transmitting their reconnaissance data instantaneously to the

F-117As and airborne control aircraft like the E-3 Sentry. Perhaps transmissions were also made to ground-based command and control centres via a satellite uplink/downlink.

Of course, as was widely reported, coalition forces suffered from time lags in transference of reconnaissance data generally and from a lack of timely bomb damage assessment (BDA) data. It can be surmised that if TR-3As were operating during the Persian Gulf War, they were few in number or were used sparingly. It should be kept in mind that, after all, only about 40 Stealth fighters were deployed to the Gulf.

Despite the origins of the THAP programme, the TR-3A's configuration suggests that it does not have extraordinary high altitude capability similar to the retired SR-71. The TR-3A is not likely to have an altitude capability beyond 45,000–60,000 feet. Also, this aircraft's top cruise speed is probably in the high subsonic range.

Accordingly, it would appear that the TR-3A's normal battlefield flight envelope is either a low, terrain-following route to the outskirts of the surveillance/target area at which time it pops up to capture an overhead or side view for its onboard sensors or a higher altitude flight profile, using powerful sensor magnifiers, and relying entirely on its stealthy design for evasion. In relaying reconnaissance data from near or over the battlefield, some form of frequency shielding must be in play. This would be particularly crucial if transmissions were being made via direct data link to incoming Stealth fighters.

Aviation Week & Space Technology reported that a full-scale aircraft with the outlines of the THAP model was sighted in May 1990 not far from the Air Force Flight Test Center at Edwards Air Force Base in southern California. It was also reported that a scaled down THAP prototype first flew in 1981 from the top secret Groom Lake, Nevada test site, the same base for Lockheed's 'Have Blue' demonstrators.

Below: A likely explanation for the emergence of the TR-3A is that Northrop, after the loss of the XST stealth aircraft competition to Lockheed in the mid-1970s (Lockheed won with its concept that ultimately evolved into its F-117A Stealth fighter), chose to further explore the possibilities for the stealth concept it had been developing. Northrop's entry in the XST competition had a twin-finned, triangular planform with the engine air inlet mounted on top of the structure immediately aft of the cockpit. This concept seems to have been refined and possibly scaled up to serve as the basis for the TR-3A, depicted in this artist's impression. The engine air inlets, like those on the B-2 Stealth bomber, are located on either side of the cockpit along the wing's upper surface. As a tactical reconnaissance aircraft, the TR-3A would provide real-time or near real-time reconnaissance to command and control centres via satellite uplink/downlink. Stealth fighters, inbound on attack missions, may receive transmissions via direct data link from loitering TR-3As. Also, the TR-3A itself may be able to acquire and strike ground targets with precision-guided munitions. Reportedly, the TR-3A is nicknamed the "Black Manta."

CHAPTER 17
JAST: Revised Attacker/Fighter

Opposite: Boeing, a partner in the Lockheed-led A/F-X team that based its design on the F-22, provides this artist's impression of the A/F-X. In this scene, two aircraft are flying very low and at high speed with wings swept. No smoke or contrails are visible. They are crossing the shore line, presumably after having launched from a carrier stationed safely distant off the coast. High overhead is another pair, possibly flying in the escort role as the A/F-X was to have an air-to-air combat capability along with its ground attack capability.

Faced with an ageing inventory of A-6 Intruders, the U.S. Navy has been quite aware of the need to replace its venerable medium attack aircraft. The carrier battle group is built around the bomb-toting Intruders — the aircraft that deliver the punch. Ultimately, the many elements of the carrier battle group, comprised of numerous support ships and a wide variety of fixed- and rotary-wing aircraft involving many thousands of specially-trained individuals, are geared to ensure that the bomb droppers, the A-6s, strike their assigned targets.

The Navy turned to a contractor team offering a highly unconventional design. Designated the A-12, the aircraft planform was a perfect triangle (not unlike the TR-3A which has a triangular planform but with rounded tips and mildly curved edges) with a topside bulge near the pointed nose marking the two-seat tandem cockpit canopy. Engine air inlets were designed to blend into the bottom of the wing on either side of the forward centre-line. Nozzles were apparently to be located on the underside and well forward of the trailing edge.

Fuel and weapons were to be carried internally. Weapon bays would open to discharge all ordnance. Clearly, the A-12 was conceived as an exceptionally stealthy aircraft. Without any vertical control surfaces, the triangular A-12 resembled a small B-2 Stealth bomber only with engine air inlets and nozzles switched from above to below and with a straight trailing edge instead of the sawtooth trailing edge.

The A-12 concept looked as if it would achieve control around all axes in flight by means of numerous control surfaces at and near the trailing edge. There may also have been long span leading edge slats. The aircraft would, after all, have to be capable of controlled low-speed approaches for

landing on carriers. It appeared that the outboard half of the wing on each side could fold for stowage.

It raised some eyebrows when the A-12 was dubbed the Avenger. During World War II, this name was applied to Grumman's carrier-qualified torpedo bomber, the TBF (also licence-built under the designation TBM). Given that the A-12's contractor team consisted of McDonnell Douglas and General Dynamics, the historic name seemed usurped.

But this matter became moot when Defense Secretary Cheney cancelled the A-12, citing higher than anticipated costs and a delayed development schedule. Shortly before the programme's cancellation, the contractor team revealed that in addition to filling the medium attack slot, the A-12 would have potential as an electronic warfare (EW) platform. (Incidentally, the EA-6B Prowler is an electronic jamming aircraft that evolved from the A6 Intruder.) In the view of the contractors, there would also be a reconnaissance role for the A-12. Most intriguing, they said the A-12 would have air-to-air combat capabilities.

Indeed, this was a harbinger for when the Navy reopened the competition, the dual roles of air-to-ground and air-to-air were specified and the aircraft's generic designation AX was changed to A/F-X (attack/fighter-experimental) to reflect the expanded mission requirements. Five contractor teams entered this major combat aircraft competition.

Not surprisingly, McDonnell Douglas and General Dynamics (subsequently Lockheed) planned to submit a revived version of their A-12. Northrop joined this team in October 1991. Its experience on the B-2 and TR-3A would have been very helpful to the further development of the A-12, which appeared to borrow heavily from both of those existing Northrop

designs. This team later withdrew from the A/F-X competition.

Lockheed and Boeing were going to offer an aircraft based on their F-22 Advanced Tactical Fighter. Grumman (now scheduled to become part of Northrop) was joined by Lockheed and Boeing in offering a 'clean sheet' design. Rockwell was teamed with Lockheed's Advanced Development Company (the Skunk Works) for a new design. Finally, McDonnell Douglas and Vought (in which Northrop has an interest) were in partnership on a fresh design.

In the meantime, the Navy's overall outlook and strategy have changed. A new philosophy as to the mission of naval aviation was espoused in late 1992. Taking into account the collapse of the Soviet Union and the dismantling of the Warsaw Pact, the Navy no longer envisions massive confrontations in the 'blue water' of the open seas. Its job today is viewed as not so much the protection of sea lanes on the world's oceans, but rather the support of coastal and amphibious operations. Naval strategists refer to these sorts of engagements as littoral conflicts.

The Department of Defense conducted a much ballyhooed Bottom-Up Review that reappraised U.S. defence needs in light of a radically changed geopolitical climate and inescapably grim budget realities. Based on the recommendations emanating from this sweeping evaluation, Secretary Aspin decided to cancel the A/F-X. In its place, a loosely defined plan for a joint service attacker/fighter was begun. This aircraft supposedly would become operational in 2012, five years later than the previously expected service entry for the A/F-X.

One idea drawing attention in the wake of the A/F-X's cancellation is the joint advanced strike technology (JAST) programme. This aircraft would be equally adept at attacking ground targets as fighting against other aircraft. As such, its design would deviate from the attack-oriented configuration of the ill-fated A-12. The JAST would take on the characteristics of a fighter, and would incorporate all the features expected of next generation combat aircraft.

A particularly notable feature that may go into the JAST's design is an advanced short take-off and vertical landing (ASTOVL) capability. It may be that the ASTOVL concept (discussed in Chapter 10) will be swallowed up by the JAST. Indeed, Boeing has proposed a multi-role aircraft that could be manufactured in two distinct versions — an ASTOVL type for the Navy/Marines and a conventional take-off and landing (CTOL) type for the Air Force. Because of modular design, both versions could be built on the same production line.

Because of the shift in strategic thinking, some observers have suggested that the JAST need not have a heavy weapons payload capacity nor a deep penetration capability. Others have gone further in view of the Navy's altered outlook and suggested that carriers would not be required at all. The long legs of Air Force assets like the B-2 would be able to deliver the necessary ordnance wherever heavy bomb loads were required, they claim.

But this argument fails to take into account the limited number of Air Force long-range heavy bombers and their inability to sustain attrition. Also, even assuming success in knocking out the distantly located targets, the requirement for support of coastal and amphibious operations may still be there. Moreover, the Air Force is itself in need of an attack aircraft to replace the F-111, the F-15E, and eventually even the F-117A. The leading candidate is the JAST.

Any aircraft expected to replace the Intruder has big shoes to fill. The A-6, now passing its thirtieth year in operational service, has performed in its assigned mission of medium attack as well as anyone could have hoped. As difficult as it has been to picture a superior replacement, the JAST, if developed wisely, should significantly surpass the capabilities of its able predecessor.

The JAST will have a stealthy design, with weaponry likely to be stored internally. Like a next generation fighter, it will be able to defend itself against the latest threat aircraft. Its speed will probably far exceed that of the A-6, perhaps going well up into the supersonic range. Because of advances in air-to-ground weapons, the JAST ought to be able to launch fire-and-forget weapons at great distance from the target, reducing exposure to enemy fire, yet achieve improved accuracy. In this way, it ought to have greater impact even though it may carry less of a bomb load.

Development of an acceptable powerplant was under way during the A/F-X programme. It must allow an extra measure of fuel efficiency to afford the JAST the necessary range and ondurance. Off-the-shelf engines do not seem up to mission requirements.

Prototypes will be developed to demonstrate the technology. Two of the competing contractors probably will be selected, and after a 'fly-off' the winning team will proceed with full-scale engineering and manufacturing. A total

Navy buy of 575 A/F-Xs was planned. The number that the Air Force would have purchased was undetermined.

Increasing budget pressures are forcing the services to squeeze every ounce of capability from new aircraft. The days of military aircraft dedicated to a sole task are quickly waning. Even an aircraft like the F-22, designed as a pure air superiority fighter, is being 're-invented' into a strike fighter.

Before the budget got so tight, there was to be a navalized F-22, referred to as the NATF (Naval Advanced Tactical Fighter). Now, the JAST itself is to incorporate fighter characteristics. By the time it enters service, it will probably be joining the F/A18E/F, the upgraded and enlarged versions of earlier model F/A-18s.

At that point, the JAST will represent the high-end and the F/A-18E/F will represent the low-end of the carrier attack and fighter mix. Interestingly, both aircraft will be compromises, aimed at fulfilling dual roles.

Below: The ill-fated A-12 Avenger is depicted in this artist's impression superimposed over a carrier at sea immediately after a catapult launch. Its flying-wing design, devoid of conventional tail surfaces, is reminiscent of the B-2 Stealth bomber and of the stealthy TR-3A reconnaissance aircraft. The pilot and bombardier were to sit in tandem in the far forward cockpit with the bubble-type canopy. Powerplants were to be located in the wing under the crew stations with the engine air inlets blended into the wing's bottom. All fuel and weapons would be carried internally to maximize stealth. Although the A-12 was cancelled, its contractor team members, McDonnell Douglas and General Dynamics (subsequently Lockheed) planned to submit a revised A-12 design in a later competition for the now cancelled A/F-X programme. The two companies were joined in October 1991 by Northrop which offered extensive experience in low observable technology with programmes like the B-2 and TR-3A.

CHAPTER 18
B-2: Return of the Flying-Wing

Long before the world was awakened to the efficacy of stealth in air combat, designers at Northrop were fashioning the B-2, a flying-wing bomber that would be virtually undetectable by enemy sensors. The idea of a flying-wing was not new to Northrop. For decades, company founder, John K. "Jack" Northrop, pioneered the development of such an aircraft. But his motivation was the belief that an aircraft consisting of essentially nothing but a wing would offer a purity of flight not attainable otherwise.

His efforts culminated in the production of a small number of jet-powered YB-49s

Right: The Northrop B-2 Stealth bomber is in many ways the reincarnation of John K. "Jack" Northrop's beloved flying-wing. Unlike the YB-49, the first jet-powered Northrop flying wing of the 1940s which was predicated on a belief in its purity of aerodynamics and inherent structural sturdiness, the B-2's design was driven by stealth. Technological advances, particularly in computers and materials, overcame the stability and control problems that plagued the YB-49 and led to its swift demise.

after World War II. Because technology, particularly in materials and flight controls, lagged behind the larger idea, these flying-wings suffered stability and control problems. Although they happened to exhibit the beneficial spillover effect of not being easily detected by radar, the flying-wing programme was cancelled.

Some 40 years later, but still before the much publicized success of stealth aircraft in raids on Baghdad during the Persian Gulf War, on 22 November, 1988, the modern day flying-wing, the B-2 Stealth bomber, was rolled out into public view. Unlike its predecessor of the 1940s, this flying-wing's design was driven by a desire to maximize stealth. Also, unlike the earlier flying-wing, the B-2 was developed in an age when technology had finally advanced enough to make a flying-wing

practicable for demanding military missions.

Stealth is an easily misunderstood concept. Most people immediately conjure up images of an aircraft that succeeds in avoiding detection with radar-evading capabilities alone. Indeed, lowering the radar cross section (RCS) is the most important aspect of a stealth design since radar has the longest range among sensors and is therefore potentially the most serious detection threat. Yet, for an aircraft to be truly stealthy it must possess low observables in a number of spectra, including not only the radar but the infrared, acoustic and visual.

While traditional techniques to counter and/or evade radar have emphasized electronic jamming of enemy radars and the use of chaff to throw-off incoming

Above: The B-2 is ordinarily flown by a two-person crew although a rear, third seat is available for future mission requirements. Both pilot positions have a centre control stick, as seen in this detailed view of the cockpit simulator. An extraordinary amount of data is integrated and displayed on full-colour cathode-ray-tube (CRT) multi-function display units (MDUs) at the pilot stations. In the centre panel is an engine performance monitor screen. There is adequate redundancy such as double sets of data entry panels (DEPs) and throttles so that if one pilot becomes incapacitated, the remaining pilot can accomplish the mission and return to base. The ejection seats may be individually activated.

Above: The first batch of B-2s is shown on the Northrop assembly line. The development of three dimensional computing combined with CAD/CAM made possible the manufacture of the B-2. Tolerances are so tight that the B-2's 172-foot wing span is accurate to within a quarter of an inch. Almost 900 new materials and processes were developed along the way in perfecting the B-2. Seeking to expand its technology base, in early April 1994, Northrop outbid a competing aerospace contractor for control of Grumman and plannned to rename the surviving company Northrop Grumman Corporation.

radar-guided missiles, the B-2, like the F-117A Stealth fighter, is designed to be inherently undetectable by radar. The B-2, in fact, represents another generation over the F-117A in radar-related stealth. At the time of the F-117A's development, computer technology had not yet progressed to where the aircraft could be designed in three dimensions. As a result,

the design of the Stealth fighter's structure is based on faceting, the employment of many interlocking panels.

Advances in computation allowed a different approach in the design of the B-2 Stealth bomber. To begin with, the B-2 has neither a horizontal nor a vertical tail surface. These typically major contributors to RCS have been eliminated altogether in the B-2. Moreover, the B-2 in cross-section has smooth, rounded shapes that reduce the possibility of strong radar returns.

Northrop designers realized the importance of eliminating as much as possible corners that form intersecting right angles, as these are known to reflect radar energy. With ordinary designs, the most notorious of these corners in terms of radar reflectivity is the point where the wing and fuselage join.

The B-2's overhead planform reveals a kind of boomerang shape. Importantly, the sweep angle of the wing's leading edge is matched by the angle of the trailing edges. This commonality of exposed edge angles significantly reduces RCS.

Electromagnetic currents from enemy radars can build-up on the skin of an aircraft. If these currents come into contact with what is known as a discontinuity, they will scatter, potentially sending a return to the emitting radar. Traditional discontinuities, such as a sharp trailing edge and uneven tolerances, have been dealt with in the B-2 design. The sawtooth shape of the wing trailing edge, repeated

elsewhere such as along the borders of the main landing gear doors, helps reduce edge scattering. Northrop, using advanced CAD/CAM techniques, achieved the highest manufacturing tolerances for any aircraft in history, ensuring that the B-2, from wingtip to wingtip, is accurate to within a quarter of an inch.

Engine air inlets are blended into the top of the aircraft's wing in two distinct humps on either side of the centreline. This on-top position shelters the potentially revealing inlets from ground radars. Rather than install shielding grids in front of the inlets as was done on the Stealth fighter, the B-2 uses S-shaped ducts to channel inlet air to its four engines.

The best means of lowering an aircraft's RCS is through its shape. But, of course, aerodynamic considerations must not be ignored. Where there is no choice but for aerodynamics to dictate shape, employment of radar-absorbing material (RAM) is a partial answer to controlling the RCS. Usually composites like fibreglass containing carbon or ferrite particles form the basis of RAM.

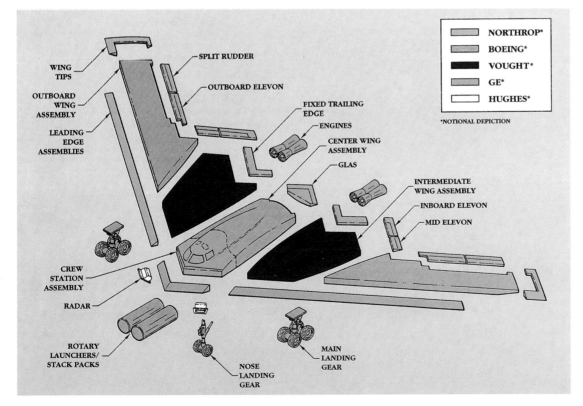

WING TIPS
SPLIT RUDDER
OUTBOARD ELEVON
OUTBOARD WING ASSEMBLY
FIXED TRAILING EDGE
ENGINES
LEADING EDGE ASSEMBLIES
CENTER WING ASSEMBLY
GLAS
INTERMEDIATE WING ASSEMBLY
INBOARD ELEVON
MID ELEVON
CREW STATION ASSEMBLY
RADAR
ROTARY LAUNCHERS/ STACK PACKS
NOSE LANDING GEAR
MAIN LANDING GEAR

NORTHROP*
BOEING*
VOUGHT*
GE*
HUGHES*

*NOTIONAL DEPICTION

Left: Northrop's four leading subcontractors among the more than 4,000 on the B-2 are Boeing Defense & Space Group, Vought, General Electric, and Hughes Aircraft. The contributions of each are depicted in this diagram. Though its size is near the smallest of the parts shown, the Hughes APQ-181 multi-mode radar is one of the most critical in making the B-2 an effective bomber. It has dual electronically-scanning antennas that are connected to high-speed signal processors. This powerful radar can be used for low-level terrain-following inbound to the target. It can also scan to the side and detect enemy aircraft. Supposedly, its advanced technology is such that while operating in this defensive mode it remains almost invisible to enemy radars. Constantly varying power and frequencies may account for this ability. The radar can also search for and detect the primary ground targets. Hughes has designed the radar with built-in test (BIT) software for ease in locating system faults.

Below: On 17 July 1989, the B-2 lifted off for the first time. The flight originated from Northrop's facility in Palmdale, California. Designated AV-1 (Air Vehicle 1), this plane had been rolled out for public viewing the preceding November. No real prototype was built. Northrop decided to proceed with full scale production models from the outset of the manufacturing process. The company and its industrial team members had accumulated more than 800,000 hours of testing prior to the first flight. All aircraft except AV-1 are slated to enter operational service as part of the 509th Bombardment Wing at Whiteman Air Force Base. In spring 1994, the Air Force chose "Spirit" as the B-2's official nickname.

The B-2's wing leading edge and probably some other unavoidable edges are made out of RAM. Reportedly, radar absorbing paint has been used to coat particular B-2 surfaces. Again, while RAM helps, it is not a total solution. Indeed, disappointing low observability results during flight tests in July 1991 apparently have been traced to the radar reflectivity of certain of the B-2's edges and surfaces.

Clearly, the main heat source picked up by infrared (IR) sensors is the engine exhaust. Historically, aircraft have ejected flares to draw away IR threats such as short-range air-to-air missiles. Military aircraft design has been sensitive in more recent years to the issue of reducing or obscuring IR emissions.

In the case of the B-2, the exhaust nozzles are rectangular, not circular. This means that in any given time frame more of the exhaust stream is exposed to the cooler outside air. The expedited mixing contributes to a faster dissipation of the heat.

The engine does its own mixing of cold bypass air and air that moves through engine hot parts. When the exhaust exits the nozzles it travels across specially fabricated heat-resistant tile surfaces. The aerodynamic airflow over the wing is designed to engage the exhaust stream at this point, further enhancing heat dissipation.

Minimizing the acoustic signature is as critical as reducing the RCS for sound can give away inbound attackers as readily as radar reflectivity. Fortunately, the exhaust flow mixing incorporated into the B-2's design offers quieter engines as a concurrent benefit. Also, typical mission profiles call for stealth attackers like the B-2 and the F-117A to fly at relatively high altitudes on the way to the target, descending to a lower strike altitude when in close proximity to the target. The high altitudes give a cushion of protection from acoustic detection.

Also, neither the Stealth bomber nor the Stealth fighter is capable of supersonic flight. The B-2's top speed is said to be in the high subsonic range. Blasting through the sound barrier, creating a loud aural footprint would hardly serve to ensure secrecy. However, as designers peer into the next century, providing supersonic

Left: As a weapons platform the B-2 is reputed to be exceptionally stable. Its conventional bomb load capacity according to the baseline plan is eighty 500 lb iron bombs, an undisclosed number of precision-guided munitions, or 36 cluster weapons. The rotary launchers/stack packs are projected to handle a much wider assortment of weapons such as sixteen 2,000 lb precision-guided bombs (eight times the bomb load of the Stealth fighter) or eight precision-guided deep penetrator munitions. The goal on all but 'bomb truck' saturation bombing missions is to enable the B-2 to launch precision-guided ordnance from a considerable distance on a fire-and-forget basis. In this way it will not be vulnerable during the time the weapons are en-route to the target.

capability for otherwise stealthy combat aircraft is likely. The future attacker ought to be able to operate in the hostile zone with impunity due to its stealthiness but have supersonic speed to exit the area.

Stealth aircraft must avoid detection by the oldest spotting method of all, scanning by human eyes. Not surprisingly, the F-117A is painted black and all of its combat missions to date have occurred at night. The B-2 is also a dark colour and would probably execute its bomb runs after sunset. The absence of vertical control surfaces makes the B-2 naturally difficult to see from the front, rear and sides.

Additional measures to reduce visual detectability include eliminating engine smoke and managing contrail formation. The B-2's engines evolved from a family of engines in modern military aircraft. As such, they have a smokeless exhaust. There is unconfirmed word that the engine exhaust temperatures are somehow regulated, perhaps in conjunction with IR suppression, to prevent the condensation that produces contrails.

Control of the B-2 is a highly complex affair. Flown by a side-by-side two-person crew (a rear, third seat is available if mission requirements so dictate), the pilot sits in the left seat and the mission commander sits in the right seat. Both positions have a centre control stick. The inputs on the sticks are read by a quad-redundant advanced electronic fly-by-wire (FBW) flight control system. The control surfaces are then deflected by the appropriate amount.

There are nine control surfaces, all along the sawtooth trailing edge. Outboard on both the starboard and port serrations are two rudders/speed brakes. Next to these surfaces on the same serrations are elevons. On the inboard serrations are pairs of aligned elevons. The elevator is the pointed tail (sometimes called the beavertail). It reacts to vertical gusts, maintaining constant pitch in cruise flight. The absence of the customary vertical control surfaces minimizes the B-2's sensitivity to sideway gusts. The requirement for bombers to be stable platforms has not changed.

This control surfaces arrangement represents changes from the original design that called for seven control surfaces. Studies and early testing showed that the additional control surfaces were necessary and that the wing needed to be reshaped and strengthened by insertion of two thick titanium spars known as carry-through boxes. A testament to the integrity of the final design is that Northrop completed structural ground testing in December 1992 by taking the wing to a factor of 160 per cent of the maximum design flight load before it broke.

Northrop and its B-2 industrial team of more than 4,000 sub-contractors are responsible for the development of almost 900 new materials and processes in connection with the Stealth bomber programme. Like most future combat aircraft, the B-2 structure is derived largely from composites like carbon fibre/epoxy for greater strength and reduced weight. Composites also allow for smoother, more perfectly shaped surfaces which contribute to stealthiness. Another enhancement of low observability is that composite structures can be joined by a cocuring process which obviates the need for fasteners

From nose to tail the B-2 measures only 69 feet, or about the length of an F-15 fighter. Yet, the aircraft's wing span is a massive 172 feet, or roughly equivalent to that of a B-52 bomber. Gross take-off

Right: The B-2 is compatible for inflight refuelling from both the KC-10, shown here with two B-2s, and the KC-135. The Stealth bomber's unrefuelled range is an impressive 6,000 nautical miles, largely because of the efficient aerodynamic flying-wing configuration. Its inflight refuelled range is extended by 4,000 nautical miles. The B-2 has global reach. With a $460 million investment at the home base in central Missouri, up to 16 B-2s should be quickly deployable at any point in time.

weight is 376,000 lb with a payload of 40,000 lb.

The four General Electric F118-GE-100 engines each produces approximately 19,000 lbs of thrust. These powerplants combined with the B-2's unusually efficient all-wing design provide an unrefuelled cruise range of 6,000 nautical miles and a refuelled cruise range of 10,000 nautical miles. The B-2 is clearly a bomber with long legs and a heavy weapons carriage capability.

A total of six B-2s will participate in the flight test programme. All of these but one will become part of the operational force. This is possible since Northrop did not build a flying prototype as is normally the case with the development of combat aircraft. Instead, the Northrop team engaged in more than 800,000 hours of testing before the B-2's first flight on 17 July, 1989. This extensive pre-flight testing was greater than for any other aircraft and has contributed to a flight test programme that experienced fewer surprises than would otherwise be the case.

In recognition of the incredible technological achievement represented by

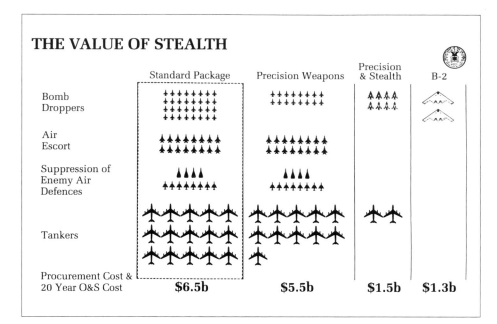

THE VALUE OF STEALTH

	Standard Package	Precision Weapons	Precision & Stealth	B-2
Bomb Droppers				
Air Escort				
Suppression of Enemy Air Defences				
Tankers				
Procurement Cost & 20 Year O&S Cost	$6.5b	$5.5b	$1.5b	$1.3b

Above: This chart shows, on the far left, a 'standard' strike package consisting of 75 aircraft used to attack a key target in Iraq during the 1991 Persian Gulf War. Reportedly, this package failed to hit the target. The package immediately to the right, involving sixteen 'bomb droppers' carrying 'smart bombs' and supported by 39 planes of various types, was sent but achieved results no better. Finally, eight F-117As, supported by only two tankers, did the job. Northrop and the Air Force like to suggest that the same mission could have been accomplished with only two B-2s. Interestingly, comparisons (perhaps biased) based on procurement costs and 20-year operating and support costs are provided at bottom. Most important is that the B-2 strike package sends fewer aircrew, a total of four pilots, into harm's way.

the design, development, and successful flying of the B-2, Northrop and its team along with the Air Force were awarded the coveted Collier Trophy in May 1992. Presented by the National Aeronautic Association, this honour is regarded as the most prestigious in the U.S. aerospace industry.

Originally, the Air Force sought to buy 132 B-2s. This number proved prohibitive due to the aircraft's high price tag in an environment of dwindling economic resources and mounting pressures for re-ordering of budget priorities given the collapse of the stalwart cold war nemesis, the Soviet Union.

Some critics charged that the B-2 would not have a mission in light of the dramatic geopolitical changes. They even suggested that with the prospect of all-out nuclear war practically eliminated, the early arguments supporting the B-2's development had themselves become obsolete. However, in reviewing the record, the Air Force, while emphasizing the B-2's deterrent role as a vital part of the nuclear triad, pointed to the B-2's versatility and potential use as a conventional bomber in its initial B-2 mission statement of 1 November, 1981.

The highly classified nature of the B-2's development probably contributed to its

perception as a troubled weapons system. The Congress and the public were wary of a defence contractor using the argument of national security to keep certain facts from view, especially when certain of those facts might prove embarrassing. Eventually, Northrop reversed its public relations course, and in the last stages of the B-2 budget debate sent company speakers around the country lecturing on the virtues of stealth generally and the B-2 in particular.

When a commitment for 132 aircraft fell obviously outside the realm of what the government would fund, an effort was made to persuade Congress and the administration to fund 75 aircraft. But this was too ambitious as well. In the end, funding was provided for a total of only 20 operational B-2s. Essentially, the decision called for purchasing the aircraft already in the production process and no more. The programme's cost cap was set at $44.5 billion.

Fixes required to cure the B-2's radar detectability are now known. It is anticipated that a B-2 unit will reach operational readiness in the mid-1990s. The only dedicated B-2 facility will be at Whiteman Air Force Base in central Missouri, currently a site for Minuteman missiles. B-2s will be operated there by the 509th Bombardment Wing.

A $460 million investment in infrastructure was made at the base in preparation for the first B-2's arrival which occurred, appropriately enough, on 17 December, 1993, the 90th anniversary of the Wright brothers' first successful powered flight. Full operational readiness of this first B-2 will not be achieved for about another two years. Because of the original emphasis on the nuclear mission, a precision-guided conventional weapon delivery capability will not be installed until 1996. The Air Force is striving to have the joint direct attack munition (JDAM) ready for the B-2 fleet at that time. All 20 of the deployable Stealth bombers being procured are scheduled to be fully operational by mid-2000.

As an example of the Stealth bomber's special needs, a fire suppression system

Above: The B-2 is powered by four General Electric F118-GE-100 turbofan engines. Developed from the B-1B's F101 engine and the F110 engine used in the F-16 and F-14, it provides fighter-like responsiveness as well as proven reliability. Each F118-GE-100 provides approximately 19,000 lb of thrust. It is non-afterburning since minimizing IR emissions is vital to the B-2's stealthiness.

built into the floor of the brand-new hangars will be able to automatically spray foam upwards to cover the underside of the massive wing, supplementing a normal hangar ceiling system that by itself would not be able to attack a fire raging below the aircraft. Failure to immediately douse an external B-2 fire could cause irreparable damage to the composite structures. The new buildings are reportedly estimated to have useful lives of at least 50 years.

In the 1991 Persian Gulf War, stealth was proven to be an invaluable asset. A small number of F-117As succeeded in knocking out heavily defended, high priority targets when in some cases much larger strike packages had failed to do so earlier. B-2 supporters have used the success of Lockheed's older stealth attack plane, the F-117A, as a linchpin in their argument.

That the B-2 will have a force multiplier effect is evident, providing, of course, that the new and much larger Stealth bomber achieves real-world stealthiness at least on the order of the F-117A. With B-2s on their way to operational service and with regional political disputes of various types all around the world seeming to errupt violently at an alarming pace, the ultimate test may not be far off in the future.

In the debate over the B-2, little attention was paid to the fact that the U.S.'s entire long-range heavy bomber force may be cut to little more than 100 aircraft and that about half that force will be more than 30 years old. Obviously, the world's lone superpower will have to rely upon that minimal bomber force making increased use of precision-guided munitions as well as upon a fleet of smaller medium and light attack aircraft for its global power projection.

There is a certain amount of attrition in the normal life span of any weapon system. This prospect does not bode well for the total force of a hundred long-range heavy bombers. With so many eggs riding in so few baskets, particularly in the case of the B-2, the destruction of even a single plane becomes a loss of critical proportions. Because of this, some observers have questioned the willingness of U.S. leaders to commit the operational B-2s to battle except in the most dire circumstances.

The B-2, a technological marvel and among the most expensive weapons systems ever produced, in an ironic twist, may lead, on a long-term basis, to reduced armed confrontation as policy makers perceive that the tools of future war are too expensive for their budgets. If this trend towards procurement of fewer but vastly more complex weapons systems continues, then logic suggests it will eventually result in the fielding of one enormously costly super plane by each of the remaining industrial alliances. Like tribal custom of the past, each side will send its chosen warrior, at the controls of their super plane, to settle the disagreement in one-on-one combat. Under such circumstances, the most modern and high-tech equipment would have a strangely primeval deployment.

109

CHAPTER 19
C-17: Globemaster Reborn

Below: The McDonnell Douglas C-17 airlifter is undergoing an intensive flight test programme at the Air Force Flight Test Center at Edwards Air Force Base. The first C-17, known as T-1 (Test-1), is shown on a flight test over the desert. The C-17 is being built for a 30,000-hour flying service life. Note how the dark green and grey camouflage paint scheme stands out against the sandy desert background. The red and white boom protruding from the nose is an instrumented probe. It was not installed on any of the other aircraft in the flight test programme.

If an imbroglio develops in some remote part of the world requiring massive deployment of U.S. forces, all eyes turn to U.S. Air Force Air Mobility Command (AMC) to get the transport job done as rapidly and efficiently as possible. Presently, AMC is reliant on the mammoth C-5 Galaxy and the voluminous C-141 Starlifter to carry troops and haul cargo to the theatre of operations and on the rugged C-130 Hercules to inject combat units and feed supplies to forward positions.

Mission planners mulled this all-Lockheed assortment of strategic and tactical airlifters, logically concluding that it would improve the transport fleet's

effectiveness to have an aircraft capable of going from the home base directly to forward positions. Or, as the aircraft's prime contractor has put it, a lifeline to the frontline.

The design settled upon and now undergoing flight test is the McDonnell Douglas C-17. The major beginning design driver was the cargo-carrying requirement specified by the Air Force. Various load combinations of trucks, armoured personnel carriers, tracked vehicles, attack and scout helicopters, cargo pallets, tanks, and troops had to be able to fit in the aircraft's "cargo box" under particular deployment scenarios.

With the dimensions of the cargo box locked in, the design team then could devise the shape of the outer structure As the Air Force was looking for a transport with short take-off and landing (STOL) capability, a high-wing configuration was chosen. Some consideration was given to an arrangement where the engines would be mounted above the wing.

Studies showed that substantially increased lift can be generated with upper surface blowing (USB). Basically, the efflux from top-mounted engines blows across the wing's upper surface, and if flaps are extended down, the flow of air remains attached to the upper surface of the lowered flaps. However, there is more drag in this arrangement which translates into a major penalty when in cruise flight. Therefore, the team opted for a conventional arrangement, like that found on the C-5 and C-141, with the four engines slung under the wing.

McDonnell Douglas did apply an innovation from its YC-15 demonstrator. It was found that short-field performance could be improved by using a powered lift concept known as the externally blown flap (EBF) system. The engine exhaust is blown into large slotted flaps enhancing lift during slow, steep approaches to landing. Further enabling short-field landings are full-span wing leading edge slats and a set of eight spoilers. Also, aerodynamic drag caused by the dramatic upsweep of the aft fuselage is tempered by canted ventral strakes.

Above: Developed initially with the Soviet and Eastern Bloc menace in mind and with the prospect of having to rapidly airlift personnel and materiel to central Europe, the C-17 is still necessary for improving airlift operations. One study estimated that if the C-17 had been available during the 'Operation Desert Shield' build-up, cargo could have arrived 20-35 per cent faster. The aircraft will be able to carry loads weighing up to 172,000 lb. The C-17 will have outboard underwing stores stations to accommodate electronics pods or aerial refuelling pods with reels.

The C-17 design is viewed generally as one that has steered clear of the radically new. Rather than experiment with untested concepts, C-17 programme managers opted, where possible, to acquire off-the-shelf technologies. The C-17 is composed of just 8.5 per cent composites by weight. Structurally, about 70 per cent of the aircraft is good old aluminium. The powerplants are a military version of the engines used on a popular commercial airliner.

In the development of the new airlifter, the McDonnell Douglas design team has, by and large, taken existing technologies and stretched them as far as they can go. Through tweaking the systems, performance benefits have been attained.

Perhaps most impressive is the C-17's projected ability to fly an unwavering five degree glideslope (compared to a three degree glideslope typical for airliners and transports) for a precision landing on an unpaved runway and come to a stop in just 3,000 feet. This remarkable performance is made possible by the aircraft's lift enhancements, a head-up display (the first for a military airlifter), a braced structure with strong landing gear, and powerful thrust reversers.

When on approach to an austere field, the HUD allows the pilot to look forward through it and see the runway as the aircraft descends at the steep five degree angle. Superimposed on the HUD is a symbol representing the touchdown aim point. By maintaining the glideslope and keeping the aim point positioned in the HUD, the aircraft can set onto the end of the short landing strip, not wasting any of the usable length.

The C-17 is expected to have an approach to landing speed of just 115 knots, compared to about 125 knots for comparably sized airliners and transports. Because the C-17 is not intended to flare before landing, as this would eat into the usable length of the runway, it will slam into the ground with a force akin to Navy aircraft landing on carrier flight decks. The C-17, supported by its Menasco-built heavy-duty landing gear, is stressed for

touch-down at sink rates of up to 900 fpm, compared to the 200/300 fpm for airliners.

The thrust reversers allow the C-17, when on the ground, to turn 180 degrees in less than 90 feet and to back-up on a two per cent grade. Importantly, the reverse thrust is directed both forward and upward at 37 degrees. This reduces the possibility

of foreign object damage (FOD) and facilitates ground crews in the performance of their tasks.

The thrust reversers are a major element in providing the C-17 with superb ground manoeuvrability. After all, in a real world combat environment, ramp space will probably be limited and cargo unloading operations will be cramped. There is also consideration being given to the use of the thrust reversers in flight for rapid tactical descents from high altitude.

The well-lighted cargo space is versatile and reconfigurable. The cargo box floor is festooned with a veritable *pot-pourri* of seat fittings and over 220 tie-down rings. The

Left: The inflight refuelling capability of the C-17 gives it global range, required for the power projection that is part of Air Mobility Command's mission. Seen here with a KC-135 tanker, the C-17 requires flight control software changes before it can comfortably refuel from this tanker type. Some notion of the C-17's size can be ascertained by how slender the KC-135 appears by comparison.

only loading/unloading point is the rear opening. There is a two-piece door, the lower portion of which is a ramp, containing the same structural integrity as the strengthened floor.

The C-17 can be configured to airlift 102 combat-ready paratroopers or 48 litter patients. In its flight test programme, the C-17 has carried an M-60 tank. The aircraft will be able to handle outsize loads like the 65 ton M-1 Abrams tank. With maximum payload of 172,000 lb and at the maximum gross weight of 585,000 lb, the C-17 will require for take-off a paved runway that is about 7,600 feet long.

Testing has shown that the C-17 falls slightly short of the already relaxed payload/range specification calling for the ability to fly 2,400 nautical miles over water with required fuel reserves carrying a payload of 160,000 lb. Of course, aerial refuelling which is possible through the aircraft's overhead receptacle aft of the cockpit, can extend range to anywhere in the world. The wing is swept 25 degrees and this contributes to the C-17's optimum cruise speed calculated at between Mach 0.74–0.76.

The airlifter has a vital airdrop capability. Clearly, there are conditions that may preclude transports from landing in an area, and airdrop is the only feasible manner of access. Paratroopers and equipment can be airdropped from the C-17. An attribute of the C-17 is its compatibility with the Low Altitude Parachute Extraction System (LAPES). With this system, pallets containing up to 60,000 lbs can be released through the opened rear ramp/door via chute extractions while the aircraft skims over the extraction zone, obviously a flat area, at no more than 10 feet above the ground.

The C-17's four Pratt & Whitney F117-PW-100 high-bypass turbofans each produce 37,000 lb of thrust. These engines are highly reliable, having accumulated in their commercial designation, PW2040, around five million flight hours powering Boeing 757s operated by airlines like Delta and Northwest.

Equipped with a full authority, fly-by-wire (FBW), quad-redundant digital electronic flight control system (EFCS), the C-17 is flown by a two-person crew. The EFCS controls 29 flight control surfaces. These surfaces move according to the inputs of the pilot and co-pilot who manipulate control sticks as opposed to control yokes traditional in transports. If more than two of the four flight control computers fail, the aircraft has a back-up hydromechanical system that automatically engages to give the flight crew a bare "return home" capability. The C-17 is the first military airlifter and the first four-engine U.S. aircraft to have a FBW system.

The FBW system was deemed necessary as wind tunnel tests showed that the C-17, owing to its massive T-tail, possessed unforgiving deep stall characteristics. With a FBW system, the aircraft is blocked from entering a deep stall. An angle-of-attack limiter system (ALS) restricts the elevator so that potentially hazardous attitudes leading to an unrecoverable deep stall are avoided. As another preventive, a stick-shaker is installed to warn of an impending stall. It should be pointed out that the high T-tail with its variable-incidence horizontal stabilizer makes a positive contribution by enhancing stability which is critical in the choppy air of low-level flight.

The C-17 has been engaged in flight test since 15 September, 1991. The flight test programme started when the first aircraft, designated T-1 (Test-1), flew the short hop from its assembly site at the McDonnell Douglas plant in Long Beach, California to the Air Force Flight Test Center at Edwards Air Force Base. The first several production aircraft, designated P-1, P-2, etc., are being used in the flight test programme. Plans call for these models to be reconfigured at the test programme's conclusion and delivered to the operational fleet.

The test programme has seen the C-17 pass some crucial milestones. As the director of the Air Force's C-17 programme office has pointed out, "The programme has flown more flight test hours in fewer days than any other large test aircraft in Air Force history." Yet, the C-17, on its way to

Opposite: The C-17 is powered by four Pratt & Whitney F117-PW-100 high-bypass turbofans based on the PW2040 used to power commercial airliners. In early C-17 flight tests, an excessive fuel burn of minor proportions was discovered. The specific fuel consumption is being modestly improved through engine modifications. The underwing nacelles each have two vortex-flow generators that protrude with a slight upwards cant just aft of the air inlets. These devices serve to delay onset of flow separation over the wing.

operational use, seems plagued by an unusually abundant string of problems.

There were highly publicized problems with improper wing riveting. An automatic riveting machine defectively installed the wing rivets. Certain apparently faulty control surfaces on the T-1 caused restrictions to be imposed in the early part of the flight test programme. Possible cuts in the carbon composite material of the elevator and ailerons during manufacture may have compromised the integrity of these control surfaces. Unrelated to these problems, fuel leaks started to occur.

These troubles, pertaining largely to manufacturing processes and procedures,

have been rectified. But still other problems afflict the programme. In a scathing report in May 1992, the General Accounting Office (GAO), a government watchdog agency, criticized the prime contractor for using the JOVIAL computer software language when the Pentagon had specified as far back as 1983 that the Ada language be used. The Air Force was criticized equally as much in the report for waiving the Ada requirement.

Sub-contractors were allowed to use the computer language of their choice, so a total of six languages was applied to the C-17 programme, leading to a situation, in the GAO's opinion, where there are likely

Above: In seeking to procure the C-17, the Air Force wants an airlifter capable of carrying the kind of load that a C-141 can carry and yet have short take-off and landing (STOL) qualities that will allow it to operate from austere fields previously the exclusive domain of C-130 turboprop transports. The third production C-17, known as the P-3, makes its first landing on the dry lake bed at Edwards Air Force Base in California's Mojave Desert. Its landing gear, rolling across the desert floor, can be seen kicking up dust.

to be "excessive software maintenance costs". It has already been determined that flight control software changes are necessary to improve the C-17's handling characteristics when being refuelled by the KC-135 tanker. (Refuelling from the KC-10 does not present the same difficulties.)

Later in the year, it was revealed that the FBW system on the T-1 aircraft disconnected during flight test. A safe landing was made using the back-up hydromechanical system. This FBW system malfunction was caused by a variance in airflow to the air data computers. The T-1 aircraft, unlike the production models that followed, has a long nose-mounted instrumentation probe that produced the disruptive airflow. The problem was solved by replumbing the air data system on the T-1.

An unexpected setback occurred on 1 October, 1992, when a C-17 wing failed during a static test conducted by McDonnell Douglas. Wanting to ensure the wing's sturdiness, contractor plans called for the wing to be tested to 150 per cent of the greatest load the C-17 would ever encounter in operations. The static test wing failed after being taken up to near

the 130 per cent mark with the wing-tips pushed by hydraulic actuators approximately eight feet above their normal position.

Naturally, flight restrictions mandating avoidance of high stress loads were placed on all flying test programme C-17s and were expected to remain in effect until the cause is isolated and a solution devised. The fractures occurred simultaneously and at equidistant points on the wing, between the engines on both sides. This symmetry in the failure was considered a promising sign that a remedy could be applied quickly and relatively easily.

The damaged wing was repaired and strengthened in anticipation of a repeat structural test. During this test, on 10 September, 1993, the wing fractured again, but only on the port side in the same vicinity as the previous port side fracture. McDonnell Douglas claimed that an average overall load of slightly in excess of the specified 150 per cent was achieved prior to the break, but Air Force officials questioned this. A blue-ribbon review panel investigated and concluded that the break occurred at 144 per cent. Obviously, some further redesign is necessary and there will be an attendant delay in the production schedule as well as an increase in programme costs.

The wing was considered a hallmark of the C-17 programme. A supercritical airfoil with 9.5 feet high outwardly-canted winglets at its tips, the wing is thick enough for McDonnell Douglas workers at the Long Beach assembly plant to routinely crawl inside as part of normal construction. Fresh air is pumped through about two dozen hoses into a given wing while workers are inside.

Wing span measures 172 feet with winglets, and wing area encompasses 3,800 square feet. Spars, stringers, and skins are made from single pieces of 7050 aluminium. The wing contains 177,000 fasteners. The aircraft is 174 feet in length and has a cargo volume of 20,900 cubic feet.

Even though no new technologies have been developed for the C-17, its planned introduction into the Air Force inventory has been a monumental challenge. Just painting the exterior of one C-17 requires 300 gallons of paint. At the Long Beach plant, about nine million parts based on 20,000 engineering drawings go into the construction of each aircraft. Certain aircraft components are put together in a building with a floor area equal to 9.5 football fields.

Joining of the constituent parts resulting in final assembly occurs in another building twice as large. This huge building, referred to simply as Building 54, has the largest floor area of any enclosed structure in California. Its floor space is a gigantic 1.1 million square feet which equates to over 25 acres. McDonnell Douglas boasts that its Building 54 could hangar 64 fully inflated Goodyear blimps.

The C-17, like aircraft programmes before it, has experienced some setbacks, but with persistence in problem solving the aircraft may yet emerge as a credible Air Force transport for the years ahead. Everyone watching would do well to remember that flight test programmes, the more rigorous the better, are supposed to find the bugs prior to operational status. Amid doubts about the C-17's capabilities that have arisen from some quarters of Congressional committee rooms, it should be noted that

an individual who should know, an Air Force test pilot on the C-17 programme, was overheard saying shortly before this book went to press that he thought the C-17 was destined to become the Air Force's next great airlifter workhorse. There could hardly be a more rousing endorsement.

With the demise of the Soviet Union and the disappearance of the Warsaw Pact threat, which was part of the rationale for developing the C-17 in the first place, Defense Secretary Cheney cut the Air Force's original buy down from 210 aircraft to 120. McDonnell Douglas pointed out that this would lead to higher unit costs.

But more recently, the Pentagon has indicated a probability of reducing its C-17 buy to as few as 50. The shortfall in the transport fleet would be filled by purchases of off-the-shelf airliners such as the 747, 767, or MD-11. There would be heavy pressure on the Air Force to buy McDonnell Douglas's MD-11 as a way to smooth over the company's losses from a dramatically scaled down C-17 programme.

McDonnell Douglas hopes to sell the C-17 to foreign users, which could lower unit costs. Expectations are for a worldwide C-17 market of from 50 to 75 aircraft. Some West European countries, Canada, and Japan have reportedly expressed preliminary interest. Successful penetration of the C-17 into the world marketplace might pre-empt the eight-country Euroflag consortium which is conducting feasibility studies on the Future Large Aircraft (FLA), a military airlifter that conceptually bears a striking resemblance to the C-17. The FLA, if pursued, would enter service no earlier than 2004.

The first operational C-17 squadron, the 17th Airlift Squadron of the 437th Airlift Wing, has already begun receiving the new transports at Charleston Air Force Base in South Carolina. Preparations are in progress for the scheduled full start-up of this unit in early 1995. If the C-17 overcomes its turbulent beginning and proves as dependable as its predecessors in the proud Douglas Aircraft (now McDonnell Douglas) family of military transports, then its newly-adopted name of Globemaster III will be most fitting.

Chapter 20
Hokum: Russian Werewolf

In 1992, the Russian Army selected the Kamov Ka-50 (NATO codename Hokum) as its new attack helicopter. The Ka-50, which is produced by the Moscow-based Kamov Helicopter Scientific & Technology Company and which first flew in 1982, competed for the Russian Army's order in a fly-off competition against the Mil Design Bureau's Mi-28 (NATO codename Havoc).

By mid-1993, it was announced that Russia had amended its earlier decision, choosing to purchase unspecified quantities of both the Ka-50 and the Mi-28. (The Mi-28, like the McDonnell Douglas Apache, has a two-seat configuration and a conventional main rotor/tail rotor system.)

In an attempt to boost export sales, Kamov signed a far-reaching production and marketing agreement with Group Vector of the U.S. As a sign of how radically the geopolitical situation has changed, the American company is headed by a retired U.S. Air Force General who directed the U.S. Defense Intelligence Agency. Kamov publicly displayed the

Ka-50 for the first time at the Farnborough Air Show in September 1992. This unveiling in Britain preceded even any public display of the aircraft in Russia.

While Russian design bureaux usually have been sanguine about accepting the codenames devised for their aircraft by NATO, Kamov has shown its independence, perhaps as a sign of new-found Russian marketing savvy, and has given its new attack helicopter the distinct nickname 'Werewolf'. At Farnborough, the Ka-50's tail was emblazoned with this nickname.

The Ka-50 is a peculiar admixture of the new and the old. Its most striking departure from today's attack helicopters is its fully articulated coaxial, contra-rotating main rotor system. This main rotor system obviates the need for a tail-mounted anti-torque rotor and provides the additional advantage of allowing the helicopter to back-up into foliage for cover.

Another innovation for an attack helicopter is the Ka-50's single-seat configuration. Building on its experience as a designer and manufacturer of naval helicopters, where minimizing pilot workload is imperative, Kamov has come up with a cockpit design it touts as futuristic. But the model on display at Farnborough did not appear to represent a significant advance in flight management systems.

The instrument panel featured an early generation moving map display, there was a head-up display along with provision for a helmet-mounted sight, avionics including an autopilot were fully integrated, and a weapons system data link allows for transfer of target information to and from other aircraft.

Unlike many new combat aircraft designs, the Ka-50's cockpit has limited window area and thereby does not afford good visibility. This seems to be a result of the efforts to increase pilot protection in the

Below: The twin-engined Ka-50 is in flight with its tricycle landing gear retracted. Note the coaxial, contra-rotating main rotor system and the heavy armament carried on the starboard stub-wing pylon — a pod with 83mm unguided rockets and launchers loaded with the Vikhr laser beam-riding anti-tank missile (ATM).

aftermath of the disastrous Soviet experience fighting against Stinger-armed Afghani mountain tribesmen. This lack of visibility could actually complicate the pilot's ability to hover low to the ground.

The cockpit shell is shielded with a steel wall over a composite core that can withstand the impact of 23mm rounds. A first for helicopter pilot protection is the installation of a zero-zero ejection seat. The Zvezda K-37 is a rocket-boosted ejection seat that when activated shoots up and out of the aircraft.

In the ejection sequence, a panel above the pilot blows off. Explosive bolts on each side of the six rotor blades ignite, separating the blades from the main shaft and clearing a vertical path for the evacuating pilot. Of course, Russian assault helicopter forces will have to modify their formations, emphasizing more of a line abreast technique to ensure clearance in the event of a pilot ejection.

The Ka-50 is powered by two Klimov TV-3117VK turboshaft engines, each producing 2,200 shp. The helicopter's infrared (IR) signature is reduced through the use of engine exhaust shielding. Because there is no tail rotor, all engine power is used to drive the main rotor. The six rotor blades are made almost entirely of composites. The rotor blades are swept at the tips.

Maximum speed in a shallow dive is 189 knots, which is impressive and probably attainable in part because of weight savings from the aircraft's single pilot configuration. Climb performance and manoeuvrability are also reputed to be equally as impressive. The Ka-50, which is 35 per cent composite materials by weight, has been designed to withstand a loading of three Gs. For maintenance purposes, the attack helicopter has been designed to provide easy access to all systems. Landing gear is a retractable, tricycle-wheel arrangement that is stressed to permit hard touch-downs.

A drawback of the Ka-50's weapons systems is the location of its single barrel 30mm 2A42 gun. The gun's placement on the starboard side of the fuselage severely restricts the gun's movement compared

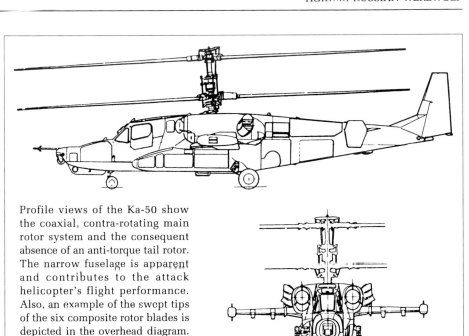

Profile views of the Ka-50 show the coaxial, contra-rotating main rotor system and the consequent absence of an anti-torque tail rotor. The narrow fuselage is apparent and contributes to the attack helicopter's flight performance. Also, an example of the swept tips of the six composite rotor blades is depicted in the overhead diagram. The tailboom sports a tailplane with endplates.

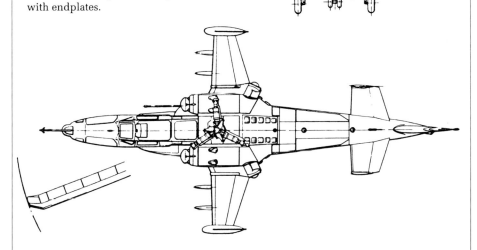

The serviceability of the Ka-50 is a boast of the Kamov design team. In this diagram, six technicians of varying specialities are servicing the helicopter simultaneously. Because the aircraft stands low to the ground and airframe panels can be used for climbing to the top of the main rotors, no special platform is required. This is obviously advantageous when it comes to field maintenance. Also, as can be seen, many sections of the Ka-50 are being accessed easily through large swing-open panels.

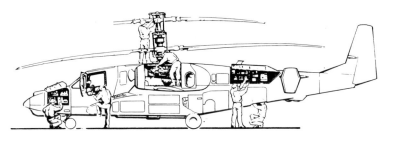

with other modern helicopter guns that are typically mounted in swivelling chin turrets. Although the Ka-50's gun has reasonable vertical movement capability, its lateral movement is restricted to just 15 degrees. If a target is at a substantial angle to the Ka-50's nose and the gun is the weapon of choice, the pilot must turn the helicopter towards the target in order to use the gun.

A variety of weapons may be carried on stub-wing pylons. The most advanced of these is the Vikhr anti-tank missile (ATM). One laser, mounted in the helicopter's nose, is used for rangefinding and the other nose-mounted laser projects a beam that the ATM rides to the target. The Vikhr is a super-sonic missile with a range of 5–6.2 miles.

The Vikhr can also be used, according to Kamov design personnel, as an air-to-air missile when the target aircraft is not exceeding a speed of 432 knots. This means that other helicopters and older close air support aircraft would be vulnerable. However, the system exposes the Ka-50 itself to attack in that its pilot must keep the laser energy focused on the target until scoring. Pods containing a total of up to 40 83mm unguided rockets also fit on the stub-wing pylons.

The most startling claim by the Kamov designers, and one that seems plausible, is that the entire tail can be blown away by enemy fire and the Ka-50 will retain sufficient stability for the pilot to make a controlled landing. Supposedly, the

Right: On public display for the first time at the 1992 Farnborough Air Show, the Ka-50 is parked amidst its armament. The side-mounted 30mm gun can be seen. Also, the small cockpit windows which restrict visibility in favour of more armour plating for greater pilot protection are evident.

helicopter was successfully flight tested without its tail. This is within the realm of possibility as the tail is not a load-bearing structure.

At Farnborough, the Russians were trying to interest the British Army in exploring the purchase of an export version of the Werewolf. Marketing directed towards other Western countries, as well as nations in the Middle East, was under way. Obviously, any Western government would need to substantially rework the design to fit Western powerplants, avionics, and weapons systems as the only means of ensuring a secure parts supply.

But of greater concern is the single-seat configuration. It is highly questionable that the Ka-50 can be effectively piloted in all scenarios by a lone individual. In a high threat environment against a sophisticated enemy at night in marginal weather when hovering near the ground, the workload on a single pilot trying to lock-on to a target and launch weapons successfully would likely exceed human limitations.

The Ka-50 does have its strengths. In a lower threat environment where the battlefield is clear of all but small arms fire and where the adversary is not highly mobile, a scenario not unlike the Soviet experience in Afghanistan, the Ka-50 would be more likely to inflict considerable damage. The Ka-50's attributes are not meager, and its official in-house nickname of Werewolf is more apt than the NATO designation of Hokum.

CHAPTER 21
Tiger: Combat Chopper

Eurocopter, the consortium of France's Aérospatiale and Germany's Deutsche Aerospace, embarked upon the Tiger helicopter programme in 1976, with governmental approval for full-scale development coming in 1987. The original plan called for France to buy 215 of which 75 would be escort/combat support/air-to-air combat helicopters, designated the HAP (hélicoptère d'appi-protection) and 140 would be dedicated to the anti-tank role, designated HAC (helicopter anti-char).

Germany was to buy 212 in the anti-tank configuration, designated PAH2 (panzer-abwehr-hubschrauber).

Budget cuts and changes in the perceived threat have caused Germany to alter its commitment. The German purchase has been reduced to 137 helicopters. Instead of being dedicated tank killers, they will be delivered in a new multi-role configuration. When the Tiger programme originated, Germany's biggest military fear was of Soviet-led Warsaw Pact forces rumbling towards its border spearheaded by columns of tanks.

As that prospect receded, the need seemed to increase for versatile hardware capable of responding in a flexible manner to a variety of missions. Also, it will probably be easier for Eurocopter to market a multi-role configuration than one dedicated to a specific task. For the time being, France's planned buy of the two types remains firm.

A possible customer is the British military which has a requirement for up to 125 new combat helicopters. British Aerospace has teamed with Eurocopter to offer the Tiger. Several other helicopters now on the world market are being offered in this competition.

The Tiger is a straight-forward attack helicopter design, devoid of surprises. It features stepped-up tandem cockpits, pilot in the front with weapons systems specialist behind. Nearly 80 per cent of the aircraft structure by weight is composite materials. The main rotor system has four composite blades and a fibre elastomeric (FEL) bearing hub. The three-bladed tail rotor is also of composite construction. Stub-wings aft of the rear cockpit provide for a considerable weapons-carrying capability. There are also external fuel tank attach points for ferry flights.

Power is provided by two MTR 390 turboshaft engines, each producing up to

1,285 shp at take-off. These powerplants, with a fully automatic digital engine control (FADEC) system, were developed expressly for the Tiger by a three-company consortium comprising Germany's MTU, France's Turboméca, and Britain's Rolls-Royce. It is expected that MTR 390 engines will find application in a number of other emerging helicopter programmes.

The Tiger's cockpits were designed to provide both crew members with excellent visibility. Large flat windows enwrap the crew stations. A 30mm chin-turreted gun is slaved to either the forward or aft helmet-mounted sight (HMS) so that the barrel will slew in the direction that the gunner turns.

Each crew station has two liquid crystal display (LCD) multi-function displays (MFDs) that provide integrated data and one control display unit (CDU) for avionics management. There is some coventional instrumentation for redundancy's sake. The helicopter can be flown from either cockpit. However, the cockpits are not identical in the anti-tank version. A cathode ray tube (CRT) is to be installed in a head-up display (HUD) for the weapons officer in the rear seat. Current design calls for this specialist to manipulate two hand grips dedicated to the operation of the advanced anti-tank missile system.

Weapons compatible with the Tiger include the Trigat advanced fire-and-forget anti-tank missile, the HOT 2 wire-guided anti-tank missile, the Mistral and Stinger air-to-air missiles, and 2.75 inch rocket pods. The HMS is the main targeting and display device in air-to-air combat, most likely against other helicopters. The HMS displays flight symbology which can be overlaid on a forward-looking infrared (FLIR) image.

The Tiger will have a night and adverse weather combat capability. Depending on the configuration, it will have either a roof-mounted or a mast-mounted sight (MMS). The sights have a low-light TV camera, a thermal imager, and a laser rangefinder.

Numerous protective features have been incorporated into the Tiger. A relatively low radar signature has been a design goal. Suppression of the IR emissions has also

been addressed in dealing with engine exhaust. Armour plating divides the two engines, serving as a preserver in the event one engine is hit in combat. Fuel tanks are self-sealing. The lower fuselage and landing gear are energy absorbent. In fact, the landing gear is stressed to withstand impacts at vertical descents of up to 6.5 metres per second. The crew seats are armoured and crashworthy. Still, the crew faces some vulnerability due to the exposure from the huge windows.

Since the maiden flight of the first Tiger prototype on 27 April, 1991, the helicopter has exhibited good handling qualities. Within about the first 100 flight hours it climbed to 13,000 feet, achieved a top speed of 170 knots, and incurred load factors up to 2.7 Gs. Design endurance of 2 hours and 50 minutes has been proven.

Without further delays, the Tiger should enter service around the turn of the century. Though not radical in design, it promises to be a solid performer. Producing a multi-role version makes sense as mission requirements can change rapidly. Confronting tanks in the deserts of the Middle East, ferreting out guerrilla fighters in the Balkan slopes, or escorting humanitarian relief workers in drought-stricken Africa are prospective tasks. Adapting quickly to the peculiar needs of each situation will be essential for any degree of success.

Above: The Tiger can be equipped with a mast-mounted sight (MMS). While hovering behind trees or brush, the MMS can remain above the foliage searching for or tracking the target. The MMS contains a low-light TV camera, a thermal imager, and a laser rangefinder. Once locked on, the helicopter can hover up a tad to fire. The two crew members have excellent visibility because of the large flat windows.

Opposite: This frontal view shows the narrow fuselage of the Tiger, a common design feature of attack helicopters that reduces their exposure to enemy fire. The stub-wings can carry an assortment of weaponry. In this configuration, the Tiger prototype is outfitted with two inboard pods each holding twenty-two 2.75 inch air-to-ground rockets and two outboard pods each equipped with two Mistral air-to-air heat-seeking missiles. Mounted at the chin is a 30mm gun capable of use against both ground and air targets. Aerial combat would probably be against other helicopters.

CHAPTER 22
MDX: Light Utility Helo

For many years, the family of Model 500 helicopters produced by McDonnell Douglas Helicopter Company (previously Hughes Helicopters) has enjoyed commercial success with sales to both civilian and military users. Seeking to build on this foundation, in the 1980s McDonnell Douglas Helicopter Company embarked on the design and development of a new, more capable light helicopter.

Originally conceived as an entry into the civilian market with applications running the gamut from offshore oil rig resupply to medical evacuation, the proposed rotorcraft was labelled the MD Explorer. Now that construction of the helicopter is under way, the military potential is being considered. In its military profile, the helicopter is referred to as the MDX. In fact, the U.S. Army, through its Utility Aircraft Requirements Study (UTARS) is reviewing needs and criteria for a new light utility helicopter (LUH).

The MDX will benefit from a few new technologies pioneered by engineers at McDonnell Douglas Helicopter Company. Chief among these is an anti-torque system devoid of the customary tail rotor. Known as NOTAR (no tail rotor), this system provides the basic anti-torque force by ejecting compressed air through slots along the tailboom, thus, replacing the helicopter's tail rotor. A rotating directional thruster at the aft end of the tailboom releases air for yaw authority.

Development of the NOTAR concept began in the mid-1970s. It finally took flight in December 1981 on an OH-6 demonstrator. Six years later, this technological achievement was recognized by the awarding of the Howard R. Hughes Trophy by the American Helicopter Society. Subsequently, the NOTAR system was incorporated into the design of the MD 530N/MD 520N series of helicopters. First operational delivery was made to the Phoenix, Arizona Police Department in October 1991.

The Army, always keen to stay abreast of technologically significant developments, is exploring the NOTAR configuration. It should be pointed out that the egg-shell-shaped AH-6 and MH-6 light attack and utility helicopters, derived from the McDonnell Douglas Helicopter Company's OH-6 Cayuse, have contributed to the success of Army operations over the last decade in Grenada, Panama and the Persian Gulf. Flown by the 'night stalkers' of the elite 160th Special Operations Aviation Regiment (Airborne) based at Fort Campbell, Kentucky, these helicopters, known as the Little Birds, have secretly performed pivotal missions.

The Little Birds are an old design. While updated with sophisticated avionics for their highly classified special operations, the basic helicopters are, in the words of the 160th's commander, "simple aircraft". In the hopes of adding to the effectiveness of this unit, two of their Little Birds are being modified with the NOTAR system in an Army research and development effort. Clear advantages will be the elimination of inflight tail rotor accidents and the anxiety that comes from the possibility of such accidents when flying nap of the earth (NOE) missions. Also, with no moving rotor at shoulder level, NOTAR increases the safety of ground personnel.

Additional NOTAR advantages over the tail rotor with its drive shafts and gearboxes include a reduction in pilot workload, superior handling qualities, reduced noise, and a lower parts count. There is a possible corresponding reduction in maintenance.

Another new technology employed on the MDX is the flexbeam rotor. This is a bearingless all-composite, five-bladed rotor system with a 33.83-foot diameter. The system entails 60 per cent fewer parts,

Opposite: In this artist's impression, two MDXs, configured for light attack, have struck a couple of tracked vehicles in the open desert, conjuring up visions of what these helicopters might have been able to do in 'Operation Desert Storm' had they been available at that time. The MDX in the foreground is launching rockets from a side-mounted pod. There is also a nose-mounted sighting device. Note the NOTAR (no tail rotor) anti-torque system which has replaced the tail rotor.

weighs less, has a longer service life, and improves flight performance. Because of its size and geometry, the rotor system generates less noise and reduces loads across the hub through a balancing of the centrifugal blade loads. In spring 1992, an intensive 12-week wind tunnel test programme at NASA's Ames Research Center validated many of the rotor system's capabilities.

The MDX is twin-engined. Powerplants available are the Pratt & Whitney PW206A, producing a maximum of 593 shp, and the Turboméca Arrius 2C, producing a maximum of 605 shp. The MDX will have superb single-engine performance, capable of flying away from an in-ground-effect hover up to 4,000 feet.

Avionics architecture is built around an advanced liquid crystal display (LCD) system known as the Integrated Instrument Display System (IIDS). Appropriate symbology on the display units will replace old-style gauges. Incorporated in the avionics will be subsystems constantly monitoring the condition of the helicopter's working parts and even automatically recording engine trends.

In the case of engine malfunctions, the displays will immediately present the pilot with essential data, helping him to cope with the situation. Maintenance will be facilitated by built-in test features and the use of portable test sets. The system will consist of line replaceable units (LRUs) so that the easily detected malfunctioning unit can be promptly replaced on the flight line.

The MDX has been designed for strength and everyday practicality. The fuselage is of coventional construction, though in certain areas composites have been used. Sliding cabin doors are a comfortable 52 inches wide. They are located on both sides of the fuselage as are individual hinged pilot doors. Landing gear is a sturdy skid arrangement with a 7.33-foot spread between the skids.

Seating will accommodate eight including a flight crew of either one or two pilots, depending on the mission. All seats are energy absorbing for added safety in the event of a hard landing. The MDX, like its

predecessors in the Model 500 family, offers excellent flight visibility. In addition to the large swept back, egg-shell windshield, there are large side and bottom panoramic windows.

For internal cargo loads, the cabin floor is flat and storage space can be increased with the removal of the six passenger seats and the co-pilot's seat. The helicopter can also be configured to carry two litters with two medical attendants on board. An external load of up to 3,000 lbs can be carried.

Performance targets call for a maximum cruise speed of 170 mph and a sprint capability of 200 mph. Maximum rate of climb is estimated at 2,900 fpm while the top vertical rate of climb is forecast to be 1,600 fpm. Range should be 363 nautical

miles while expected endurance is 3.6 hours. The manufacturer says that the hourly direct operating cost will be a miserly $336 in 1992 dollars.

In its role as an Army light attack/utility helicopter, the MDX would seem to offer a simple, reliable, and relatively low cost ($2.8 million base price in 1992 dollars) alternative. Certainly, the MDX's lineage in the Model 500 family augers well for the possibilities of the new helicopter. The MDX possesses enough new technologies to make it competitive in the battlefield of the next century, but at the same time it remains a fundamentally conservative rotorcraft with the attributes of simplicity and maintainability.

The MDX makes a versatile platform in that its spaciousness would allow it to transport small numbers of commandos to critical areas or fly gunship missions. Many of the Army's weapons systems are compatible with the chopper, making it a potentially lethal fighting machine.

McDonnell Douglas Helicopter Company's ambitious FAA certification programme for the Explorer civilian version has fallen behind schedule. Certification is currently anticipated for October 1994. Design changes have been dictated by early tests or suggested by prospective customers. Among other things, the changes call for a redesign of the nose, elongating the mast by eight inches, and improving the efficiency of the NOTAR fan which is located between the two engines above the cabin.

Left: A relative of the MDX and a building block in the history of its development is this MD 530N, emblazoned in a military camouflage paint scheme. This series of rotorcraft was the first to employ the revolutionary NOTAR system.

CHAPTER 23
Comanche: Multi-Talented Warrior

Below: A Boeing-Sikorsky RAH-66 Comanche mockup in a desert camouflage paint scheme blends into the landscape of a sandy plain. The Comanche is the U.S. Army's next generation reconnaissance/attack helicopter. The proposed purchase of 1,292 Comanches will replace about 3,000 ageing helicopters that lack the new aircraft's capabilities.

In 1985, during pursuit of the U.S. Army's LH (light helicopter) contract, the Helicopter Division of the Boeing Defense & Space Group joined forces with the Sikorsky Aircraft Division of United Technologies to form the 'First Team'. Three years later, the Boeing-Sikorsky partnership and a competing group, led by a venture of Textron's Bell Helicopter and McDonnell Douglas Helicopter, were chosen for the demonstration/validation phase.

On 5 April, 1991, following scrupulous analysis of the two entries, the Army selected the design offered by Boeing-Sikorsky. This winning LH design was designated the RAH-66 (reconnaissance-attack helicopter). It was quickly dubbed the Comanche in deference to the native Americans who proudly and fiercely defended themselves.

No flying prototypes of the finalists had been built; the Army's decision was based on data accumulated through computation, simulation, and system demonstration. Ironically, the two companies comprising the losing team have extensive experience

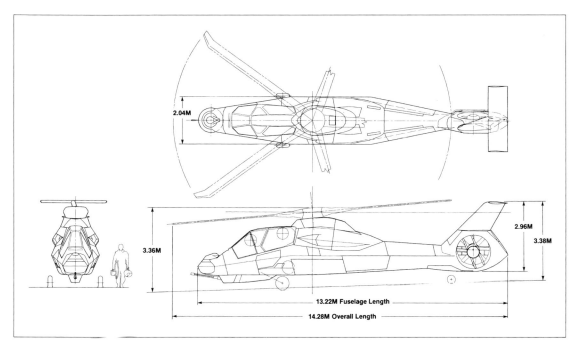

Left: The Comanche's dimensions show that it is a compact helicopter. Its fuselage width of approximately seven feet gives the Comanche a narrow frontal profile, making it a more streamlined helicopter. The RAH-66 is unusually sleek and tapered for a helicopter.

in the design and manufacture of attack helicopters, notably the AH-1 Cobra and the AH-64 Apache, respectively, while the winning team's production experience is based largely on cargo and utility helicopters like the CH-47 Chinook and the UH-60 Black Hawk, respectively.

To be sure, there were significant differences in the two competing designs, such as the vastly contrasting anti-torque systems. Yet, at the time of its decision, the Army expressed confidence in the ability of both designs to meet or exceed the published performance specifications and to excel in the envisioned LH missions of armed reconnaissance, attack, and air-to-air combat. It was reportedly the projected lower operational and support costs for the First Team's design that became the deciding factor in the Army's contract award.

The Comanche represents a genuine leap to the next generation in attack helicopters, much as the U.S. Air Force's F-22's embodiment of advanced technology promises to make it a true next generation fighter aircraft. With this helicopter conceived from scratch using a clean slate, an airframe was devised that for the first time incorporates significant low observables in a rotary-wing attack aircraft.

Like the F-22, the Comanche will have an internal weapons storage capability. This means that its missile-seeker heads may remain unexposed until shortly prior to launch. The panels of the weapons bays can open in just three seconds. Further reducing the Comanche's radar cross section is its retractable landing gear. Of course, an added benefit is the resulting aerodynamic streamlining.

The exhaust from the twin turbines will be diverted to limit the vehicle's heat signature. Moreover, the powerplant itself incorporates such design features as a narrow profile to minimize frontal area and a compact length of only 33.3 inches (847 mm) that assists in infrared (IR) suppression. In future air warfare, helicopters spearheading the battle will have to employ stealth, and the Comanche's designers have wisely taken this into account.

The newly-developed engine for the RAH-66 is the 1,200 shp T800-LHT-800, a product of LHTEC which is a joint venture of Allison and Garrett. The engine is amazing for its simplicity. It has significantly fewer parts than a conventional helicopter turbine engine, and can be serviced in the field with a mere six hand tools.

Among the First Team's ten primary subcontractors is Deutsche Aerospace (through its unit, formerly named Messerschmitt-Bolkow-Blohm) which is contributing its bearingless main rotor (BMR) technology, already tested on its BO-108 prototype. The Comanche's five-bladed composite BMR, combined with the fan-in-fin or fantail anti-torque system, successfully flight tested on the S-76 demonstrator, give the helicopter virtually unprecedented manoeuvrability. It will be able to turn 180 degrees while hovering in just 4.7 seconds and to snap turn at 80 knots in just 3.0 seconds.

These flight characteristics, enhanced by a triple redundant fly-by-wire (FBW) flight control system (FCS), will make the Comanche a more formidable combat aircraft with the flight crew enjoying the agility required to quickly home-in on ground targets and to out-manoeuvre a variety of air threats. At the same time, the fantail permits the Comanche to sink its tail boom to within a hair's breadth of natural foliage to gain the greatest advantage from masking.

The high-tech wizardry that is at the heart of the Comanche in no way compromised simple common sense. In fact, the Comanche's design seems to be an exceptional blending of the advanced and the practical. The Comanche's airframe, which is all composite, is structured in a way to allow maintenance personnel to access and service the innards by climbing on the exterior panels without the necessity of ladders or platforms. This is an important advantage, particularly in the almost assuredly inhospitable environment of the forward staging fields near the battle where the Comanche is likely to be deployed.

Further relieving the maintenance burden is the fact that the Comanche's modular units are not located one behind the other. Systems are being designed so that when a malfunction occurs it will be rapidly diagnosed and isolated through an elaborate electronic annunciator display. Only the defective portion of the distressed unit will have to be removed and replaced.

There are many access panels on the airframe which reduces the mechanic's time getting to and fixing the problem.

While the Comanche will be flyable with a single pilot, the workload may increase in certain scenarios, requiring a flight crew of two. Ensuring ease of training as well as of maintenance, the Comanche's two tandem configured cockpits are identical. Each cockpit will feature two flat panel displays known as display electronic units (DEU) on which the pilots can call up any data relevant to their mission at a given point in time.

The pilots will be outfitted with helmets linked to the DEU, providing vital readouts and images at eye level regardless of which direction the pilots' heads are turned. Kaiser Electronics is leading the development of this helmet-integrated display sighting system (HIDSS).

The First Team's avionics package represents the single most far-reaching advance for the programme. Critical avionics elements will be brought together in an integrated communications, navigation and identification avionics (ICNIA) system. Navigational accuracy will be enhanced and the pilots' navigational chores will be simplified with the inclusion of a new three-dimensional digital map display. As is a given with the emerging crop of new combat aircraft, this helicopter will have very high speed integrated circuit (VHSIC)-based signal and data processors.

Based on its experience developing such sensor-targeting systems as the target acquisition designation sight/pilot night vision sensor (TADS/PNVS), the low altitude navigation and targeting infrared system for night (LANTIRN), and, in partnership, the Longbow 'fire-and-forget' missile system, Martin Marietta is developing the Comanche's aided target acquisition/designation (ATA/D) system and its radar. The targeting system will consist of a second generation focal-plane-array forward-looking infrared (FLIR), low-light-level TV, and a laser range-finder/designator.

The Comanche is a highly adaptable weapons platform. When stealth is

paramount, the Comanche will use its weapons bays for internal carriage of its weapons payload. In this configuration it can carry four Hellfire and two Stinger missiles. If all-out attack is the mission requirement, then in 20 minutes the Comanche can have stub-wings attached to accommodate a far heavier weapons load. In the maximum missile armament configuration, the Comanche can carry up to 14 Hellfires or 18 Stingers or 62 2.75 inch rockets. The Comanche may even be able to carry the Sidewinder, in addition to the Stinger, for air-to-air combat. Of course, at all times it will have its lightweight, turreted 20mm, two-barrel Gatling gun capable of firing 750 rounds per minute at ground targets (1,500 against aerial targets).

The stub wings can also be fitted with two 460-gallon fuel tanks for ferry flights (or as the Army likes to say, self-deployment). These external tanks give the Comanche an impressive estimated range of 1,260 nautical miles. Nevertheless, the Comanche has been designed so that it can be loaded in the venerable C-130 Hercules transport in only 13 minutes. Up to eight Comanches can be airlifted by a C-5 Galaxy.

While the original award was to be for 2,096 of the new helicopters, the total has been reduced to 1,292. This quantity may be further reduced because of budget pressures or the programme may be stretched over a longer contract life. At the

time of the award to the Boeing-Sikorsky team, programme plans called for first flight in September 1994, initial operational delivery in December 1998, and completion of the Army production by 2008. At the peak, 120 Comanches would be built per year.

Since the Comanche is the Army's first all-metric aircraft and since it represents such incredible advances, it is hoped by members comprising the First Team that their product will find a large market overseas. The value in current dollars of the Army's total buy, including all phases of development and production, was expected to exceed $33 billion. However, budget pressures prodded the Army in early 1993 to instruct the contractor team to cut total programme costs by a third.

The Army estimates that in the coming two decades it will have to replace almost 3,000 ageing AH-1s, OH-6s, and OH-58s. The proposed 1,292 Comanche helicopters, flying in a complementary capacity with the AH-64s currently in the inventory, will, though fewer in number, actually, as a force multiplier, enhance the Army's combat capability while reducing operational and support costs. Significantly, the Comanche is being designed to accommodate future technological advances so that it may continue to serve as a frontline combat aircraft into the middle of the next century.

Above: This cutaway exposes the 500-round ammunition belt that feeds the 20mm turreted Gatling gun in the chin. Also shown is the nose-mounted electro-optic target acquisition/designation system that includes a second generation forward-looking infrared (FLIR) piloting and targeting sensor system, television sensor, and laser designator. As can be seen, the stepped-up rear cockpit gives the pilot in the back seat unobstructed forward vision. The eight-blade fan-in-fin or fantail tail rotor is visible.

CHAPTER 24
Osprey: Dexterous Performer

Below: The first Bell-Boeing Osprey prototype painted in high-visibility white and red flight test colours, makes a routine conversion from helicopter to aeroplane mode. The three-bladed prop-rotors are 38 feet in diameter, which represents a compromise to give reasonable performance in both modes of flight. The prop-rotors are of fibreglass/graphite construction.

The dream of a manned air vehicle that can take-off, land, and hover like a helicopter while also being able to fly as high, far, and fast as a fixed-wing aircraft is not new. As early as 1950, the U.S. Air Force solicited designs for a convertiplane. Five years later, in answer to the call for a convertiplane the Bell XV-3, a unique aircraft featuring a tiltrotor concept, flew for the first time.

For helicopter flight the tiltrotor's wingtip-mounted rotors pointed up while for flight in the aeroplane mode its rotors converted, or tilted, to the horizontal. In the course of the 11-year flight test programme, the XV-3 made 110 full conversions.

In 1958, the year that the XV-3 made its first inflight conversion from helicopter to aeroplane mode, Boeing's entry in the

convertiplane arena, the VZ-2/Vertol 76, made its first full inflight conversion. In contrast to Bell's approach, the Boeing design was based on the idea of a tiltwing whereby the entire wing shifted between the horizontal and the vertical. Sustaining lift during conversion proved difficult, and it was determined that the tiltrotor configuration is the more efficient.

Based on the promising progress achieved by the first fledgling tiltrotor, along with subsequent dynamic model tests and engineering studies, in 1973 Bell received a contract for two tiltrotor research technology demonstrators, designated the XV-15. First flight occurred on 3 May, 1977. Two years later, the XV-15 made its first full conversion. Proving the speed advantage of a tiltrotor, the XV-15 established a new speed record for rotorcraft on 17 June, 1980 when it reached 301 knots during level flight with its proprotors (as the propellers/rotors of a tiltrotor are called) tilted forward.

Recognizing the possibilities of a practical tiltrotor as well as the need to upgrade battlefield aerial mobility, the U.S. Department of Defense established the Joint Service Advanced Vertical Lift Aircraft (JVX) programme in 1981. In order to effectively tackle the programme's challenges, Textron's Bell Helicopter and Boeing's Helicopters Division (then Boeing Vertol) joined forces, announcing their collaboration on 7 June, 1982.

In 1985, as the Bell-Boeing team proceeded with design work, the JVX was officially dubbed the Osprey, after the large and agile member of the hawk family. Also, the aircraft was given the designation V-22. It was perceived primarily, although not exclusively, as a Marine Corps troop transport and the leading candidate for the service's medium lift replacement (MLR) aircraft.

The Osprey is nothing short of a revolution in aeronautics. Building on the achievements of the earlier XV-3 and XV-15 tiltrotors, it has emerged as a truly remarkable hybrid. It is far more capable than its tiltrotor predecessors, largely because of three enabling technologies:

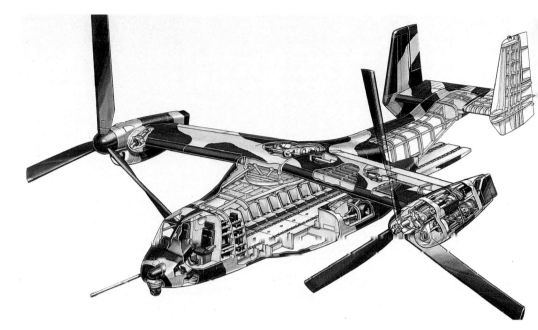

advanced tiltrotor aerodynamics, digital avionics/fly-by-wire (FBW) flight controls, and graphite-epoxy-composites. With the improvements afforded by these technologies, the Osprey is the long-awaited miracle aircraft capable of real-world helicopter/aeroplane flight.

Graphite-epoxy solid laminates comprise most of the Osprey's structure. The main advantage of such advanced composite materials is that they reduce weight while increasing strength. Moreover, these materials, when compared to traditional metals, are less prone to corrosion, can better withstand small arms fire, and tend to be more fatigue resistant.

Two bulbous sponsons protrude from the lower cabin, one on either side. These voluminous bulges are designed to carry 1,228 gallons of fuel supplemented by another 787 gallons in self-sealing tanks in the wing. The port sponson houses the aircraft's environmental control system (ECS) which, by providing an over-pressure in the cabin, protects against the fall-out from nuclear, biological, and chemical (NBC) agents.

An amazing safety feature is that the Osprey's configuration and comparatively light weight, due to composite construction, permit flotation in seas with winds of up to 25 knots and waves as high

Above: The cutaway shows the Osprey's rear, fold-down cargo-loading ramp. Also shown are some of the 12 per side, energy-absorbing, impact-resistant folding troop seats. The nose protrusions include the fixed inflight refuelling boom, the AN/APQ-174 multi-mode radar (pointing straight out), and the AN/AAQ-16 forward looking infrared (FLIR) sensor. Note the thin but wide diameter stainless steel ring, called a carousel, located atop the cabin at the wing's centre section. For stowage aboard ships, the wing swivels around this ring.

Above: A not uncommon instrument panel for future combat (and commercial) aircraft, the Osprey's cockpit is dominated by four large multi-function full-colour cathode ray tubes (CRTs). There is, of course, a conspicuous absence of traditional dial-type gauges. The few visible on the far right are for flight test purposes.

as seven feet. In water, the wingtip nacelles serve as stabilizing pontoons.

The Osprey's drive system, not without some correctable defects discovered in the flight test programme, promises to provide utterly astounding performance. The engines are mounted in the wingtip nacelles. These massive nacelles, connected to spindles, are tilted by jack screw actuators activated by flight crew control inputs. This is the heart of the tiltrotor system.

In the event that one engine should fail, a sensor automatically activates an interconnecting drive shaft that evenly distributes power from the remaining good engine so that the nagging problem of asymmetric thrust in twin-engined aircraft with a disabled engine is a thing of the past. If this were not enough, the gearboxes are pressurized, precluding moisture or grains of fine sand seeping in and causing severe maintenance difficulties. This is an especially useful design feature for deployments to desert environments like the Persian Gulf.

The aircraft's two powerplants are Allison T406-AD-400 turboshaft engines. While they are capable of producing 6,150 shp, the Osprey's transmissions are rated at from 4,200 shp to 4,570 shp depending on the specifications of the end user. In single-engine operation the maximum thrust is 5,920 shp.

Derived from the tried and tested T56 used on the C-130 Hercules and the P-3

Orion, the T406-AD-400 was built on a reliable technology base. The new engine benefits from numerous improvements such as digital electronic controls. An internal auxiliary power unit (APU) allows self-starting. This obviously enhances the Osprey's ability to operate from remote areas.

The hot exhaust gases emitted from the Osprey's engines are separated from the fuselage, somewhat limiting the IR signature. In helicopters the engine exhaust tends to wash down and cover portions of the fuselage, increasing the IR signature.

Also, because of the outboard placement of the engines and transmissions, the Osprey's occupants are safer in a crash. The proprotors are designed to avoid impacting the crew and passenger compartments should battle damage cause them to detach while in motion. A helicopter's powerplants and rotor blades are situated atop the cabin and can more easily penetrate.

Contributing to the Osprey's combat prowess is its ability to fly in the helicopter mode projecting up to 75 per cent less noise than that typically generated by some helicopters. For special operations at night, this low acoustics feature provides a notable advantage.

As is a given for modern combat aircraft, the Osprey's flight control system is fly-by-wire. Heavier mechanical linkages are replaced by a system that carries computer-generated signals based on the pilots' control inputs to hydraulic actuators that change the position of the control surfaces — the elevator, rudders, and flaperons. This system, vital to the safe operation of the aircraft, is triply redundant.

Among the innovations is a hydraulic system designed to operate at the high pressure value of 5,000 psi. Accordingly, smaller hydraulic lines than customary are installed with resultant weight and space savings.

The Osprey's cockpit accommodates two pilots. (The standard mission calls for a crew chief to be aboard.) Extraordinary protection is provided by what the Bell-Boeing team labels an anti-plough bulkhead that would absorb the energy of a forward impact. The flight deck's visibility is superb all around because of a number of big forward, side, overhead, and low-cut windows.

Standard practice is for Marine and naval aircraft to approach ship from the port side so the Osprey's pilot sits in the right seat and the co-pilot in the left seat. Air Force and Army versions, if procurred, are likely to have a more conventional seating arrangement.

When the Osprey transitions between helicopter and aeroplane modes, the cockpit flight controls automatically change from the type used to control one form of aircraft to the other (i.e., cyclic and collective for the helicopter mode and control stick and rudder pedals for the aeroplane mode). This automatic changeover ensures a manageable workload for the flight crew.

The two pilots do not have a single stand-alone gauge to read. Instead, the instrument

Below: In December 1990, Ospreys No. 3 and No. 4 performed successful shipboard compatibility tests in conjunction with the Marine Corps modern amphibious assault ship LHD-1, the USS *Wasp.* This is aircraft No. 3 about to touch-down. The standard approach from the ship's port side calls for the Marine and Navy versions of the Osprey to be commanded from the right seat.

panel is dominated by four multifunction full colour cathode ray tubes (CRTs). All critical data, such as altitude, airspeed, and engine temperatures, are displayed on the CRTs. At the push of a button on two centre-mounted digital data processor control display units (CDUs), the flight crew can call up virtually any piece of information pertaining to the aircraft's operations and scan readouts of the desired systems.

Avionics include dual mission processors, a dual 1553B data bus system, secure voice communication systems, and a wide array of navigational systems such as digital map displays. The Osprey will be able to operate in all weather conditions and at night. For protection against enemy threats, the Osprey will have radar and IR warning systems as well as chaff/flare dispensers.

Since the Osprey was conceived as a shipborne aircraft, stowage of its three-bladed, 38-foot diameter, fibreglass/graphite proprotors and wing was an essential design challenge. An ingenious solution allows the proprotors to fold inboard after which the wing, in a clockwise motion looking from above, can pivot 90 degrees around a thin but wide diameter stainless steel ring set atop the main cabin.

This procedure, which takes only 90 seconds and is automatic, results in the wing coming to rest above and in line with the airframe. When in the stowed configuration, the Osprey's width dimension shrinks from its normal 84.6 feet (the wing span in flight position) to a mere 17.3 feet.

Designed initially with an eye on the Marine Corps medium lift requirements, the Osprey can carry up to 24 combat-equipped troops or 20,000 lb of cargo internally or 15,000 lb of cargo in a sling using its dual external cargo hooks.

When serving as a fully-loaded Marine assault transport, it is projected to have a range of 500 nautical miles. Unlike military helicopters that often have to be air- or sea-lifted to the theatre of operations, which in some cases requires additional time for disassembly/reassembly, the Osprey can self-deploy with the use of auxiliary fuel tanks that extend its range to an impressive 2,100 nautical miles.

A key advantage over traditional rotorcraft is the Osprey's speed, which in the aeroplane mode is more akin to that of a fixed-wing twin-engine turboprop than a helicopter. With reasonable fuel efficiency, the Osprey can maintain a maximum cruise speed of 275 knots. When necessary, it can achieve a dash speed of 300 knots.

In recognition of the strides made in the development of this special aircraft, the Bell-Boeing team received the U.S.'s top award for the greatest aeronautical achievement of the year, the Robert J. Collier Trophy. The award was presented in May 1991 for the aircraft's demonstrated success in 1990.

Rarely, if ever, has there been an aircraft promising possibilities as diverse as the Osprey. The Osprey will not only be able to replace the ageing fleet of Marine Corps CH-46 and CH-53 helicopter troop transports, but it can perform a wide range of duties for all branches of the U.S. armed forces. However, for now budget constraints virtually rule the Osprey out for all but the Marine Corps.

In addition to the 507 Ospreys, designated the MV-22A, planned for the Marine Corps, the original programme called for the Army to acquire 231 units, also designated the MV-22A. These were to be used for medevac, special operations, and combat support. The Navy's procurement was to be 50, designated the HV-22A, for combat search and rescue, special warfare, and logistics support. An anti-submarine warfare version, known as the SV-22A, was also considered. The Air Force mulled a buy of 80 Ospreys, designated the CV-22A, for missions by special operations forces.

Still more military applications of the tiltrotor have been postulated by the Bell-Boeing team. A scaled down version of the Osprey could be used as a gunship. It would have greater speed than traditional helicopter gunships which might make the difference between victory and defeat given

Opposite Top Right: The two successful XV-15 tiltrotor technology demonstrators, one of which is seen here in flight test, paved the way for the V-22. The XV-15 research programme validated the underlying tiltrotor concept. The Osprey prototypes now flying are in many ways larger and more technologically sophisticated clones of the XV-15s.

Opposite Below: As the No. 3 prototype eases closer to the deck of the *Wasp*, Osprey No. 4, in a Marine Corps camouflage paint scheme, can be seen parked on the edge of the deck in its stowed position, proprotors folded and wing pivoted, reducing the aircraft's width to a meagre 17.3 feet from the normal 84.6 feet (the wing span in flight position).

the increasingly hazardous conditions faced by aircraft flying low over the modern battlefield.

A much smaller, unmanned tiltrotor could be used for a variety of missions such as real-time or near real-time reconnaissance. In fact, in July 1993, Bell started flight testing a maritime unmanned aerial vehicle (UAV) tiltrotor called Eagle Eye.

Additional roles for the Osprey extend to Coast Guard search and rescue (SAR). With the Osprey's multiple capabilities, the Coast Guard's operation of this hybrid could reduce, if not eliminate, five different aircraft types in the current inventory. There would be sizable long-term savings through the simplification of SAR execution, supply, and maintenance.

A fleet of Ospreys dedicated to drug enforcement could at last provide

Above: Bell is leading an international corporate team developing an unmanned aerial vehicle (UAV) based on tilt-rotor technology. Called Eagle Eye, this UAV, if accepted by the U.S. Navy, would be ship-based and provide over-the-horizon surveillance and targeting for surface combatants. In this artist's impression, an Eagle Eye is shown crossing the shore line flying low and at high speed, presumably to avoid detection, as a sister UAV hovers offshore. Safely in the distance is the mothership. Flight tests of two proof-of-concept models began in July 1993.

authorities with the technological means to effectively detect, track, intercept, and apprehend those who transport illegal substances by air. The myriad roles for the dexterous Osprey also include humanitarian relief missions, off-shore oil rig re-supply, and environmental clean-up. In each case, a tiltrotor would likely perform the task more efficiently than conventional alternatives.

An element often overlooked in the debate over government funding for the Osprey is the tiltrotor's significant potential impact on commercial air travel. Major airports throughout the U.S. and Europe are almost uniformly overcrowded. Building more multi-billion dollar full-fledged hubs, like Denver's new airport, makes sense in some cases. But, for much less expenditure, vertiports to accommodate the Osprey can be built.

Because of the Osprey's vertical take-off and landing (VTOL) capability, the vertiports could be constructed in close proximity to downtowns. With its outstanding single-engine flight characteristics, the Osprey ensures an unprecedented level of safety for flight over populous areas. Importantly the Osprey's

quiet acoustic footprint means it would meet with less community opposition.

Recognizing the beneficial impact of a civil tiltrotor, the FAA has pledged to co-operate in the certification process. Since the Osprey incorporates a novel concept and new systems, the FAA understands that it too must be innovative in its regulatory role. The rules governing the tiltrotor's civilian use will have to be written along the path to certification.

If budget concerns are allowed to thwart the Osprey, the technological infrastructure of the U.S. would suffer a mighty blow. In the current globally competitive environment, other nations would probably enter the void.

Indeed, an omen was the comment by Japan's Minister of International Trade and Industry who, upon seeing the Osprey, said, "If you produce this aircraft, I guarantee you we will buy it; if you do not, I guarantee you we will build it." At the moment, a consortium of five European companies under the Eurofar banner has studied the possibility of producing a civil tiltrotor and Ishida of Japan, having hired some experienced Osprey researchers from Bell, moved ahead with development of a civil tiltwing known as the TW-68. (The Ishida venture was mothballed in 1993.)

Some noteworthy blemishes in the Osprey programme to date have occurred in flight testing. When aircraft No.5 took off from Boeing's Wilmington, Delaware test facility on 11 June, 1991, it immediately became unstable. Despite the attempts of the pilots to steady the aircraft, it tipped to one side and impacted the ground. Though the Osprey was destroyed, no one was seriously hurt.

Subsequent investigation found that two of the three roll-rate sensors were reverse-wired. Thus, the one that was properly wired was 'out-voted'. It was revealed that earlier Osprey prototypes had also been incorrectly wired. However, these previous mistakes in wiring involved a single channel. The two good channels overrode the bad channel. Of course, these examples of faulty wiring in the earlier aircraft were corrected once discovered.

The explanation for the cause behind this potentially injurious or even fatal mishap brings into question the quality control exercised by the contractor team. At a time when the Osprey programme is under heightened scrutiny because of a shrinking defence budget, slip-ups at the factory are the last thing that should happen. Most importantly, test pilots who fly newly-rolled-out aircraft should not have to contend with the added burden of doubtful quality control.

On 20 July, 1992, an accident occurred that did result in fatalities. The No.4 aircraft plunged into the Potomac River during approach to landing at the Quantico, Virginia Marine Corps facility. Tragically, all seven individuals aboard the Osprey perished when it crashed.

It appears that either lubricating oil or hydraulic fluid leaked into the right engine housing, eventually igniting and thereby causing the right engine and the interconnecting drive shaft to fail. Remedies being considered include a modification that would automatically remove fluids from danger areas of the engine nacelles and a bolstering of the existing firewall between the engine and the transmission. Also, an entirely new drive shaft made of metal and able to withstand higher temperatures may replace the existing composite drive shaft.

Coincidentally, one of the XV-15 tiltrotor demonstrators that had accumulated 616 flight hours since 1977, crashed on 20 August, 1992 only a month after the No.4 Osprey was destroyed in an accident. While no one sustained serious injuries in the crash of the XV-15, the aircraft was severely damaged. The investigation has traced the cause to a loss of control stemming from nothing more than a loose bolt in a connecting rod.

None of the tiltrotor accidents was caused by a critical flaw in the tiltrotor concept. Instead, each of the causal factors was or can be corrected with relative ease, allowing the flight test programme to proceed albeit with only three Osprey prototypes instead of the five as planned.

In a new twist of the ongoing procurement intrigue, the Defense Acquisition Board announced in late 1992 that it was actively seeking alternatives to the Osprey for the new Marine Corps medium lift aircraft. Some of the alternatives under study are upgrades of existing helicopters, including a service life extension programme for the CH-46. The Board also accepted a recommendation that combat search and rescue as well as special operations be dropped from the requirements for this aircraft.

A draft of a revised operational requirements document has surfaced which reduced the original cruising speed requirement from 250 knots to 180 knots, eliminates the self-deployment requirement altogether, and increases the sling load requirement from 8,300 lbs to 10,000 lbs. These new requirements would have the effect of reducing the unit cost of the Osprey and allowing for a mixed replacement fleet of tiltrotors and pure rotorcraft. In fact, with the revised requirements, the Bell-Boeing team has already computed a possible per unit cost reduction of $5–7 million.

Military analysts and policy planners, mindful of the defence budget cuts now under way, should realize that the often talked about idea of simplifying operations and controlling costs through adoption of a lesser number of versatile aircraft types for multiple missions must now, of necessity, be implemented. The Osprey is a logical leading candidate to fulfil part of that objective.

With all that the tiltrotor offers and with the Osprey having come so far, it is to be hoped that this amazingly capable hybrid, expensive though it may be, is not cancelled in a budget-cutting frenzy. The tiltrotor promises to revolutionize the world of flight; it is just too valuable to discard.

CHAPTER 25
Stopped Rotors: X-Wing and Rotor/Wing

The longstanding challenge to devise a flying vehicle capable of shifting between helicopter and fixed-wing flight whilst airborne was addressed by the Sikorsky Aircraft Division of United Technologies Corporation in the mid-1980s with the Rotor Systems Research Aircraft (RSRA)/ X-Wing. Using an S-72 airframe modified with the addition of a variable incidence stub-wing and two General Electric TF-34 turbofan engines in nacelles mounted on pylons protruding from the top sides of the fuselage, the specially fabricated four-bladed main rotor system was designed to stop in flight and become an overhead X-shaped fixed-wing. In this configuration, the aircraft would be able, in theory, to achieve high subsonic speeds.

Flight tests of the X-Wing, as this aircraft was ordinarily called, occurred first with a standard five-bladed main rotor system of an S-61 Sea King helicopter. These tests examined the aircraft's flight characteristics and handling qualities in the helicopter mode only. On 2 December, 1987, the modified S-72 flew for the first time, without a main rotor at all, to test the fixed-wing flight characteristics only.

In this configuration, it was a fixed-wing aircraft (that just happened to have a helicopter fuselage) propelled by the turbofan engines. Due to the absence of a main rotor with the attendant diminution in drag, the aircraft achieved much higher speeds than typical for helicopters. Eventually, the aircraft reached 301 mph configured in this way.

The primary technological hurdle to making the X-Wing concept a success was maintaining lift while stopping the main rotor blades in flight. A proposed solution was to circulate compressed air around the blades as they began to slow on the way to stopping. The air would be emitted from

Right: The Rotor Systems Research Aircraft (RSRA)/X-Wing produced by Sikorsky in the mid-1980s featured an S-72 airframe with two overhead General Electric T-58 turboshaft engines to power the main and tail rotor systems and two outrigged General Electric TF-34 turbofan engines to provide thrust for fixed-wing flight. The specially-fabricated four-bladed main rotor system was designed to stop in flight, forming an X-shaped fixed-wing for aeroplane-like forward flight at a speed up to three times that of a conventional helicopter.

Left: On 2 December 1987 the RSRA/X-Wing flew for the first time without a main rotor to test the fixed-wing flight characteristics. This successful flight originated from the NASA Dryden Flight Research Center at Edwards Air Force Base and lasted 40 minutes. Previously, the aircraft had flown with a standard S-61 Sea King five-bladed rotor system to test flight characteristics in the helicopter mode only. The RSRA/X-Wing project, while at one point supported by NASA, the U.S. Army, and the Advanced Research Projects Agency (ARPA), and while based on the worthy stopped-rotor principle, preceded the enabling technologies. In 1988, the project was cancelled.

slits in the blades themselves. The four main rotor blades would lock in predetermined positions forming an X-shape with the two forward blades swept ahead at 45 degrees and the two rear blades swept aft at 45 degrees.

The twin General Electric T-58 turboshaft engines powering the main and tail rotor systems could then be shut down with the two added TF-34 turbofan engines taking over, providing thrust like the engines on any conventional fixed-wing jet aircraft. The targeted forward airspeed for stopping the main rotor in flight was a fast 196 mph. The projected top speed for the X-Wing with rotors stopped was 518 mph, roughly three times as fast as conventional helicopters.

Recognizing the potential offered by the X-Wing concept, this research project was supported by NASA, the U.S. Army, and the Advanced Research Projects Agency (ARPA). New technologies would have to be applied to this radical vehicle. Indeed, composites were extensively used in the main rotor blades.

Left: In this artist's rendering, the McDonnell Douglas Helicopter Company's canard rotor/wing (CRW) is firing a missile at a ground target. Note the down-words direction of the canard surfaces. In the upper right corner the two CRWs with rotors stopped can be seen speeding through the sky, their overhead planforms exposed. The two-bladed rotor when stopped in flight forms a fairly conventional wing, subject to being set at oblique angles for greater speed. The horizontal tail surface with outwardly-canted tips has almost as much span as the stopped rotor. The same two engines power the rotor and provide the thrust for flight in the fixed-wing mode. The single-seat CRW would have a weapons payload of 3,000 lb.

These four blades had a radius of 28.8 feet. They were three feet in chord with a hollow sleeve bonded to a rigid graphite "I" beam.

Despite some innovations, the X-Wing did not have at the time of the research programme all of the technology necessary to make it viable. It was truly an aircraft ahead of its time. The X-Wing, based on the worthy idea of the stopped rotor, was cancelled in 1988.

A newer variation on the stopped rotor theme has recently germinated in the design offices of McDonnell Douglas Helicopter Company. Picking up where the X-Wing left off, the McDonnell Douglas Helicopter Company concept calls for a twin-engined, two-bladed main rotor, no tail rotor vehicle with moving canards and a long span fixed tail surface sprouting large outwardly-canted tips.

Known as the canard rotor/wing (CRW), the design has gone as far as a 13-foot-long wind tunnel model. Early wind tunnel tests and computer modelling indicate that the full-scale aircraft would have a top speed exceeding 375 knots. A smaller, unmanned aerial vehicle (UAV) version with a single engine would have similar speed possibilities.

An enabling technology of the CRW is a proposed reaction drive system for both lift and propulsion. Engine exhaust gases would be vented through jets at the edge of the rotor blades providing rotation and helicopter-style lift. During conversion to the fixed-wing mode at around 150 knots, the horizontal surfaces of the canards and the tail would begin to take over some of the lift requirement. In fixed-wing mode, the same engine(s) provide the propulsion. The reaction drive system obviates the need for a transmission, which in turn provides a significant weight and maintenance savings.

A perennially troubling issue confronting designers who have wrestled with the design needs of convertiplanes is that the optimal size of a rotor blade/wing in helicopter mode is not the optimal size in fixed-wing mode. Generally, a longer rotor blade is more efficient in helicopter mode while a shorter wing is more efficient for high-speed flight in the fixed-wing mode. The McDonnell Douglas Helicopter Company design team has wisely explored the data base on oblique wing research, and suggested that the CRW's rotor blades/wings have a variable oblique angle capability for high-speed fixed-wing cruise.

It is believed, based on earlier NASA flight tests of an oblique wing demonstrator, that altering the angle of the wing in relation to the fuselage can increase an aircraft's speed. Setting a wing at oblique angles can render speed-related benefits enjoyed by swept wing aircraft. Being able to vary the oblique angle in flight, in the same way that certain existing aircraft like the B-1 and F-14 can change the sweep of their wings in flight, gives the CRW a wider performance envelope.

The CRW is most plausible as a light attack aircraft and as an UAV. The Navy is funding some preliminary CRW research, and it may be the impetus for a later programme that leads to development and production of an aircraft with a practical stopped rotor system. First flight of a prototype is planned for mid-1994.

Below: This artist's impression shows a single-engine unmanned version of the CRW. Weighing only 1,627 lb with a payload capacity of 200 lb for reconnaissance sensors, this CRW could be launched from and retrieved on flat decks of seagoing vessels. The expected speed, range, endurance, operability and serviceability of this aircraft make it of interest to the U.S. Navy.

CHAPTER 26
Tactical Missions: Mighty Copters

In June 1980, European Helicopter Industries (EHI) was formed by Britain's Westland Helicopters and Italy's Agusta. The focus of this joint venture company has been the development of the EH 101, a helicopter in the medium lift class having three distinct variants — military transport, naval configuration, and civil operations type known as the Heliliner.

Recognizing the increased importance of air mobility on the modern battlefield and the need to be able to react quickly to world crises, the EH 101 is shaping up as an impressive prospective tactical troop and cargo carrier. It can transport up to 30 fully-equipped troops in its large, unobstructed cabin. It can accommodate a combination of wheeled vehicles, artillery, and personnel. It can also be configured to carry up to 16 litter patients.

The maritime variant has been cleared for day or night operations in weather as severe as 50 knot surface winds and known icing conditions. The British Royal Navy ordered 44 of these helicopters in the anti-submarine warfare (ASW) configuration under a separate contract with IBM (coupled with Westland) as the prime contractor. This ASW rotorcraft, called the Merlin, will be fitted with a round radar antenna on the fuselage underside just aft of the retractable nose landing gear. It will also be equipped with an active dipping sonar, sonobuoy dispensers, and an onboard sensor processing suite. Britain, to fulfil its needs for support helicopters, plans to also purchase a small number of EH 101s (along with Boeing Chinooks) for the Royal Air Force.

The EH 101 incorporates a number of cutting edge technologies such as the Active Control of Structural Response (ACSR) system that cancels out a large measure of vibration by using automatically-activated hydraulic actuators as a balancing mechanism against common flight-induced vibration. An electronic instrumentation system (EIS), consisting of eight displays, provides data on a need-to-know basis so as to keep the workload manageable for the two pilots. Three engines power the helicopter, options being either the General Electric CT7-6 or the Rolls-Royce Turboméca RTM 322.

In 1992, when it looked like the programme might collapse for lack of international sales, Canada ordered 50, of which 35 were for shipborne maritime patrol and 15 for search and rescue. In the autumn of 1993, facing an anaemic economy and intense political pressures, the government reduced its order to 43 aircraft. But the newly elected Canadian Prime Minister, upon assumption of office, honoured his campaign pledge to cancel the EH 101 order. Italy intends to buy 16 ASW variants and has an option for eight more. There is an anticipated worldwide market for 800 of these helicopters in the various configurations.

Sadly, the second of nine EH 101 prototypes crashed in Italy on 21 January, 1993. All four crew members on the flight test mission were killed in the accident. Authorities are investigating the cause.

Below: The British Royal Navy's version of the EH 101 is known as the Merlin. It will have an anti-submarine warfare (ASW) capability as well as the flexibility to be configured for other naval missions such as the anti-surface vessel (ASV) warfare role. This aircraft, in part because of its advanced composite rotor blades, is able to lift 35 percent more weight and fly more than 40 knots faster than the aged Sea Kings currently being operated. Mission endurance may extend up to five hours. Each EH 101 contains up to 18,000 individual wires which translates into nearly 50 kilometres of cabling. Note the underside radar antenna. The EH 101 flight test programme began in October 1987.

Above: A mockup of the NH-90 in its naval version, known as the NATO frigate helicopter (NFH), will be capable of performing the ASW and ASV missions. Shown here with an inert Exocet missile, the display emphasises the helicopter's potential lethality with its ability to utilise such a destructive anti-ship weapon. Note the incomplete main rotor blades.

More than half the total planned flight test hours for the EH 101 programme had already been accumulated. Despite the crash, the ASW versions for the British Royal Navy are still expected to be delivered beginning in mid-1996.

On 1 September, 1992, after much study and preliminary design work, the NH-90 programme was formally launched. A consortium of Eurocopter France, Eurocopter Germany, Italy's Agusta, and Fokker of the Netherlands (subsequently acquired by Deutsche Aerospace) formed NATO Helicopter Industries (NHI) which is managing the programme.

Two basic variants are planned for this twin-engined, medium size rotorcraft — the tactical transport helicopter (TTH) configuration for army use and the NATO frigate helicopter (NFH) configuration for naval use. Available powerplants will be the same as for the EH 101, either the 2,090 shp General Electric CT7-6 or the 2,145 shp Rolls-Royce Turboméca RTM 322.

The aircraft's structure will be all-composite. Flight controls will be fly-by-wire (FBW). An automatic health and usage monitoring system (HUMS) will keep track of aircraft systems and promptly report any malfunctions. Mission endurance should exceed 2.5 hours for the TTH and four hours for the NFH. Operations, day or night, in 45-knot surface winds are a programme objective.

The TTH is being designed to carry up to 14 combat-ready troops. A rear ramp will be offered as an option to facilitate swift ingress/egress of equipment such as wheeled vehicles. The ramp would also permit paratroop airdrops. Payload capacity is estimated to be 4,400 lb. Cruise speed is projected at 140 knots, with a possible sprint capability of 160 knots.

The NFH's primary missions will be ASW and anti-surface vessel (ASV) warfare. In these roles, it will be outfitted with a variety of sophisticated sensors and weapons. At the same time, it will be adaptable to such other missions as search and rescue. Given the drag from externally mounted sensors and weapons, cruise speed is projected to be around 120 knots.

The countries of the four partner companies are expected to buy up to 726 NH-90s. The worldwide market for this helicopter is believed to be 1,200 units. First flight is scheduled for the end of 1995. Five prototypes are planned for an extensive flight test programme that should allow production deliveries to start by the end of 1999.

The Boeing Model 360 Advanced Technology Demonstrator is being internally funded as a means by which the Boeing Helicopters Division can study new technologies applicable to its current and future rotorcraft programmes. The Model 360 has a configuration in general outline similar to the well-known CH-47 Chinook. Yet, the demonstrator is really quite different. To begin with, more than 68 per cent of the demonstrator's structure by weight is composite materials. This provides a weight savings and a strength advantage.

Composites are also incorporated in the four-bladed tandem rotors and in the rotor hubs. Power is provided by two Textron Lycoming 5512 turboshaft engines each generating up to 4,200 shp. These engines and their air inlets are blended into the aircraft's structure, providing aerodynamic streamlining. The tricycle landing gear retracts, adding further to a "clean" flight configuration.

The two pilots enjoy excellent visibility because of the huge windows wrapped around the cockpit. The instrument panel has six multifunction displays, presenting data as needed to prevent excessive pilot workload. The avionics may accommodate FBW or flight-by-light (FBL) flight control systems.

On 10 June, 1987, the Model 360 flew for the first time. During ongoing tests it achieved a top speed of 214 knots in level flight, which represents a record for a helicopter of its size.

The Sikorsky Aircraft unit of United Technologies Corporation has proposed a new helicopter that borrows features from its well-regarded SH-60 and CH-53 rotorcraft. Called the S-92, this new design would be offered in both military and civil versions. The military model would be aimed at fulfilling the airlift requirements for the Marine Corps amphibious assault mission and the U.S. Navy's vertical replenishment mission.

When it comes to Marine assault, the MV-22 Osprey, with its revolutionary tiltrotor technology, would outclass any conventional helicopter of equal size, but the S-92 would be much less expensive having an estimated unit price of just under $14 million in 1991 dollars. At the same time, because of the incorporation of certain advanced technologies, the S-92 would represent a significant leap in capabilities over existing medium lift helicopters.

Designed for a flight crew of three (two pilots and a crew chief), the S-92 could transport 22 fully-equipped combat troops within a radius of up to 200 nautical miles. Because of a rectangularly shaped cabin there is an open aisle space of approximately 18 inches between the seated troops which allows the crew chief unhindered access throughout the cabin. Interior cabin dimensions are five feet and 11 inches wide, six feet high, and 19 feet and two inches long.

It is estimated that the S-92 could carry a payload of up to two tons and still have a three-hour endurance. Power will come from two upgraded General Electric T700 engines.

A large ramp located at the rear of the cabin enhances rapid ingress/egress. Facilitating this process are main landing gears that can raise the aft fuselage 18 inches when the helicopter is parked on the ground. Since shipboard operations are contemplated, the S-92's aft tail boom section may be folded sideways and the main rotor blades may be folded back over the fuselage.

Until its unveiling in late 1991, Bloomfield, Connecticut-based Kaman Corporation quietly developed the K-MAX. A cargo-hauling helicopter aimed primarily at the commercial market, the K-MAX has potential applicability to military roles. Conceived as a medium/heavy lift platform, it has special appeal to the logging industry of the Pacific Northwest where transporting timber by air may be more economically and environmentally sound than cutting truck paths through forests.

While capable of carrying up to three tons by sling, the single-engined K-MAX is not a huge helicopter. It addresses the market's need for a helicopter that can carry significant though not gigantic loads more cost effectively than enormous helicopters.

Below: The Boeing Model 360 Advanced Technology Demonstrator is used to verify technologies for current and future helicopter programmes. It has the trademark Boeing tandem-rotor configuration in which the forward rotor turns counter-clockwise as viewed from above while the aft rotor turns in a clockwise direction. The demonstrator makes extensive use of composite materials and has a streamlined structure which contribute to faster speeds in level flight. Its avionics are adaptable to fly-by-wire (FBW) or fly-by-light (FBL) flight control systems.

which is now locked in, calls for a single pilot. Instrumentation and flight controls will not be exotic. For safety, the pilot will have a newly-developed energy-absorbing seat and cyclic stick. Visibility will be enhanced by the cockpit's wrap-around windows.

The K-MAX's maiden flight occurred on 23 December, 1991 at the Kaman facility in Connecticut. Flight testing has proceeded as expected, but it was determined that the rotor blades should be lengthened by six to seven inches. FAA certification was anticipated by the end of 1993 with first deliveries hoped for in early 1994.

Clearly, the K-MAX could be used by the military for transporting loads such as equipment and ordnance. It has obvious potential as a shipborne platform. Moreover, the K-MAX in an unmanned version could be used for communications, surveillance, and environmental clean-up. As mission requirements dictate, the unmanned helicopter's dimensions could be scaled down. It is projected that with minimal external load, the K-MAX can remain aloft for up to 15 hours.

The U.S. Department of Defense reportedly financed a portion of the K-MAX's development. During the early development stages, the helicopter was known generically as the multi-mission intermeshing rotor aircraft (MMIRA).

Above: The Sikorsky S-92 draws from the best of the company's SH-60 and CH-53 military helicopters. Planned as a shipboard transport, the S-92, as depicted in this mockup, has a folding aft tail boom section as well as main rotor blades that fold back over the fuselage for stowage. The rear ramp allows for rapid ingress/egress. The aircraft has a spacious rectangular cabin that can accommodate up to 22 fully-equipped combat troops. The cockpit's wraparound windows provide the flight crew with outstanding visibility.

The K-MAX uses a unique side-by-side intermeshing counter-rotating "synchro-lift" rotor technology reminiscent of the rotor system employed on the late 1950's vintage Kaman H-43 Huskie, a U.S. Air Force rescue helicopter. This rotor system obviates the need for a tail rotor so that all the power from the proven and reliable Textron Lycoming T5317A-1 gas turbine engine goes to the all-composite main rotors for lift. The engine is derated from 1,800 shp to 1,500 shp. It is expected to operate for long periods at the maximum power setting.

Referred to by the manufacturer as an aerial truck, the K-MAX design is simple and rugged. The production configuration,

Right: Undergoing flight test, the Kaman K-MAX promises to be a popular medium/heavy lift helicopter, especially for the logging industry. Its side-by-side intermeshing contra-rotating 'synchro-lift' rotor system is similar to that used by the Kaman H-43 Huskie of late 1950s vintage. The K-MAX may find application to military missions. It could serve as a cargo hauler of equipment and ordnance. An unmanned version could also fill a number of military roles.

INDEX